SLING YOUR HOOK

Cliff Parker has been described as Angling's Number One Humorist. As he's often been called worse, he's prepared to settle for it.

Born in Manchester so as to be near his family, Parker was eventually moved on by the Keep Britain Tidy people and now lives in Amersham, Bucks, with wife, two children, insane cat and permanent overdraft.

Hobbies are fishing, frog fancying and working towards sainthood. Ambition is to be locked in a pub with Brigitte Bardot.

In SLING YOUR HOOK, Cliff Parker strikes again with his funniest fishing stories from *Angler's Mail.*

Also by Cliff Parker in Sphere Books:

THE FISHING HANDBOOK TO END ALL FISHING HANDBOOKS
HOOK, LINE AND STINKER
THE COMPLEAT WALLY ANGLER

Sling Your Hook

CLIFF PARKER

SPHERE BOOKS LIMITED
London and Sydney

First published in Great Britain by
Sphere Books Ltd 1985
30–32 Gray's Inn Road, London WC1X 8JL

TRADE
MARK

Set in Baskerville

Printed and bound in Great Britain by
Cox & Wyman Ltd, Reading

Contents

About this book

Sling Your Hook is based on the best of Cliff Parker's regular features in *Angler's Mail*, to which publication our thanks are due.

Who could forget such stirring angling sagas as 'Ollie and Stan meet the werewolf', 'I was a Sagger Maker's bottom knocker for the FBI', 'Hokamapokus and the Indian death lock', 'The curse of the cosa nostril', and 'A pain in the psst-psst-psst . . .'?

Pardon? Anyway, there's lots more where they came from, including extracts from the historic journals of that world-famed fishing club, the Sludgethorpe Waltonians.

This is angling laid bare: at last the secrets are revealed of what *really* goes on on the bank. Which makes it a book no angler can afford to be without. The same goes for any woman unfortunate enough to have a close relationship with, or even be married to, an angler. Now you'll know what he really gets up to, and why he comes home in the state he does. What's more, you'll be able to spot the fibs a mile off.

Sorry about that, lads

A funny thing happened on the way to the space ship

I have been doing some research lately into angling humour, mainly because I could use a few laughs now and again.

I started with Number One Son.

'What's the oldest fishing joke you know, me old fruit?'

'You, Dad.'

Ooh, he's sharp is that lad. But docking his spends took the smile off his face.

My researches showed that angling jokes have a significant common denominator: they're all terrible.

It set me wondering where old jokes came from in the first place. Who makes them up? Through the centuries they've been the same old jokes, bent a bit, polished here and there, or roughed up here and there. But they must have started somewhere: someone must have sat down and thought them up.

Ancient cave man joke:

'Who was that unconscious lady I saw you dragging back to your cave last night?'

'That was no unconscious lady. That was my unconscious wife.'

Another ancient cave man joke:

'Do you believe in clubs for women?'

'Yes. Big ones.'

Ug.

While I was pondering all this, I read an interesting science fiction story by Isaac Asimov. (Ancient science fiction author joke: 'Does Isaac ever change his underpants?' 'Yes. He Asimov twice a week.') The Asimov story – for God's sake get on with it, Parker – is about a scientist who wants to find out the origins of the corny old jokes. So he feeds them into a giant computer. (This is in the twenty-first century, when computers can do more than give you wrong gas bills and make you redundant.) The computer comes back with the answer: the jokes came from Outer Space.

It had decided there was no logical reason why people should find jokes funny, involving as they did so many embarrassing, sick or violent situations. It worked out that the jokes had been planted, ages ago, by beings from another planet. By observing the reaction of human beings to the different jokes, they could find out how the human mind worked, and so be prepared for the Great Takeover.

Let's help the little green men on their way by seeing what you think of this lot. Angling jokes, they are. In case you don't recognise them.

* * *

'Poor old Noah. All that water and he couldn't do any fishing.'

'Why not?'

'With only two worms?'

* * *

Two anglers were fishing on the canal when a funeral passed over the bridge.

One of them stood up, took his cap off, and waited in silence until the cortège had passed.

'What did you do that for?' asked his mate. 'Did you know the deceased?'

'Aye,' said the first one. 'And she were a good wife to me.'

* * *

Another sicky:

Funeral of the wife of a keen angler. On top of the coffin lay a rod and two cans of bait.

'Harry,' said his mate, 'I didn't know your wife was keen on fishing.'

'She wasn't,' said Harry. 'But I've got a match at half past three.'

* * *

Little lad, fishing on the corner of the street. In a bucket of water.

Vicar comes along, sees that there's only water in the bucket, and asks kindly, 'What are you doing in that bucket, young fellow?'

'Fishing,' says the little lad.

'Of course, of course,' says the vicar, thinking the poor little chap's right off his trolley and giving him a shilling. 'And how many have you caught today?'

'You're the fourth.'

* * *

In similar vein, as the vampire said to the bishop, there was the bloke who fished the National match and didn't catch a thing. But he was crossing a bridge over the river, stretching his arms as wide as they would go, and singing:

Twenty-one today...
Twenty-one today...

A steward saw him and said, 'Look here, you, you're the world's worst fisherman. I watched you all the way through the match and you didn't catch a thing. Yet you're walking across the bridge holding your arms out and singing "Twenty-one today". If there's one thing I can't stand, it's a liar. Would you mind explaining yourself?'

The angler picked up the steward and threw him over the bridge into the river.

Then he walked on, singing:

Twenty-two today...
Twenty-two today...

* * *

Two blokes going fishing.

'I'll bring the gear,' says one. 'You see to the refreshments.'

The second bloke turns up on the bank with two loaves of bread and twelve bottles of Scotch.

'What do you think you're playing at?' screams the first. 'I ask you to bring the refreshments and you turn up with two loaves of bread and twelve bottles of Scotch! What the hell are we going to do with all that bread?'

* * *

The strange thing about fishing jokes is that there are very few naughty ones. (No sex, please: we're anglers.) Among the nearest you will get to naughties are.

'I caught a mermaid last week. What a figure!'

'What were her vital statistics?'

'38-24 – and 92 pence a pound.'

Or:

Two anglers meet in a pub. One has his head bandaged, his arm in plaster and is walking on two sticks.

'By gum, you're in a bad way,' says his pal. 'What happened?'

'The wife beat me up when she found out about that weekend fishing trip.'

'How come?'

'She found out I didn't go.'

Or:

Bloke fishing out at sea pulls in a beautiful mermaid. He looks at her for a few minutes, deep in thought, then throws her back.

'Why?' asks his mate.

'How?' says the angler.

Or:

'My wife's run off with my best friend.'

'I'm sorry to hear that. What are you going to do about it?'

'I'll just have to go fishing without him.'

* * *

Lying, failure and boasting figure largely in angling jokes. (Let's face it, they figure largely in angling.)

Angler on holiday says to a local yokel, 'I can't understand it. I was told there was trout fishing in this river. But I've been here a week and I haven't even seen one.'

'Arr,' says the yokel. 'There *was* trout fishin'. But a feller came down here a fortnight ago and caught it.'

* * *

'So you want to join our angling club? Do you tell lies?'

'No. But I can soon learn.'

* * *

There was the bloke who was taken to hospital after a two-hour struggle with a twelve-pound pike which got away.

He strained himself in the pub trying to illustrate the size of it.

* * *

One angler got so used to exaggerating that he even lied about the size of his bait.

* * *

'I caught a great pike today. Twelve inches.'

'What's so special about that? I've caught lots of pike of twelve inches.'

'Between the eyes?'

* * *

Finally, there's the one about the bitterly disappointed angler. He'd spent all day flogging himself to death. Pounds and pounds of groundbait. Pints and pints of maggots. Not a nibble.

He sat in the pub that evening, trying to forget what had never happened, and staring at a huge stuffed fish in a glass case behind the bar.

At closing time the landlord prised the angler off his stool and steered him towards the door.

The angler took one last despairing look at the monster in the glass case and yelled: 'Whoever caught that fish is a bloody liar!'

* * *

If those creatures from Outer Space have been watching the reactions of you lot as you've been reading through this lot, they're going to be very puzzled indeed.

Wake UP at the back there!

Chancing my arm

I started the Coarse Season in a bad way. Poorly. Disabled. Fit for nowt. My casting arm had seized up.

I'm not quite sure what caused it, but it could well have been the Do-It-Yourself activity.

At the end of last Season we'd moved into a new house. It wasn't really new, it was sort of . . . what's the word? Old. And it needed a few things putting back onto it, such as a roof.

I was lying on the settee, my eyes closed tight in concentration, designing a new wormarium for the Parker herd of pike-strangling lobs.

'You're not spending three months lying on that settee,' said Dearly Beloved.

'Did you chirp, my little wren?' I asked, doing the W.C. Fields bit.

'I did,' she said. 'You're doing some jobs around the house.'

So it had finally come to this. If word got around I should be ostracised at the *Knacker's Hammer*. Treated with scorn and disdain at the *Duck and Pullet*. Drummed out of the darts team at the *Boot and Slipper*.

I managed to keep the secret in the pubs, attributing the scars from saws and chisels to falling downstairs and being run over at a traction engine rally. But there was no escape from the jobs, any one of which could have put my arm out.

Still, there I was on opening day, down on the canal at first light, fishing gently away, smiling through the pain and generally minding my own business. When along came these two swans.

I've nothing against swans. The most graceful and noble of birds, they are. So long as they're in somebody else's swim. In *my* swim, I hate 'em to pieces.

Still, I hef vays off makink zem schift. First, one or two friendly, pleading words. A few sterner admonitions and hisses, like 'Pssst! Off!' Then, if nobody's listening, some loud and naughty words. Finally, the half-brick. Not to hit them, you understand. Just to make the point that I'd rather they went elsewhere.

It may have been throwing the half-brick which finally put my arm out: the old flex and flick were definitely not what they used to be. But it worked. The swans hissed off.

The ripples from the half-brick subsided. The float was back in the water, the groundbait back on the bottom, and all was right with the world. Then –

'Vroom... vroom... coming into attack! Pow pow pow! Perdanggg. Under enemy fire! Taking evasive action! Weeee-yowwww...!!!'

Approaching at high speed down the canal was a little destroyer, its decks bristling with guided missiles. Swooping over it, making it swerve from side to side, was a very noisy propeller-driven aeroplane.

This is the last time I touch Mad Mac's bathtub peach wine, I thought. But most apparitions have their logical explanations. And there they came along the opposite bank: two spotty and knocky-kneed, but very brainy-looking kids. Each carrying a remote control radio set.

'Weeeeyowwww...'

'Look lads,' I called, ever so politely. 'I'm trying to fish. Would you mind just –'

'Ah, shurrup, you silly old twit!'

So much brain and so little respect for their elders.

'I'll give you silly old twit if I get across there.'

'Yah, but you can't, can you? Stupid old duffer! Fire one! Yeeeeyowwww!'

Just as the renowned Parker self-control and mildness of language was about to blow, help arrived. From a most unexpected quarter, as they say in *Clichés for All Occasions*. The swans.

They came flapping and splashing back up the cut, straight for the boat. The pair of them hammered hell out of it, pecking it and bashing it with their wings.

Lovely swans. At 'em, old buddies. Kill, fellers, kill...

Spotty and knocky-kneed little Brainchild Number Two, rot his socks, grasped the situation immediately. He brought his plane into the attack and buzzed the swans until they finally turned and hissed off upstream. But those two lovely birds had done their bit. The boat lay quiet, listing a little and bobbing in the swell left by the fracas, slap in the middle of the canal.

'Waaah!' yelled spotty and knocky-kneed Brainchild Number One. 'My boat's conked out! Can you get it, Mister?'

'I'll try,' I said. Good job I'd got my bobbly hat on, or they'd have seen the horns sprouting through my flowing locks.

A poke around the back of the towpath revealed a brick. A whole one this time.

'Wassee doing?' whispered spotty and knocky-kneed Brainchild Number Two.

'Going to make a splash,' said spotty and knocky-kneed Brainchild Number One. 'Wash the boat back here.'

One for the money. Two for the show. Three to be ready and – Eeeeyowwww ... sperLOSH!!!

The boat went up into the air as if it had been depth-charged, and came down in a massive belly flop.

'You old twit!' shouted spotty and knocky-kneed Brainchild Number One. 'You nearly hit my boat with that brick!'

'I'm sorry about that,' I said. 'But I've got a bad arm.'

I had, too. I really had.

It's not like me to miss.

Why do we do it?

Staggered back from a wet day's fishing. Soaking wet, frozen stiff, coughing, wheezing and at the point of death. Stopped off at the *Boot and Slipper* to dry out. Save Dearly Beloved having all that wet clobber around the house. There's considerate for you.

Stood in front of the fire in the Public Bar, steaming and ignoring complaints from the crib school that I was blocking the heat and causing a pong. There's inconsiderate for you, but my need was greater than theirs.

The door opened and in walked two strange lady persons. (Strange, not in having two heads or anything unusual like that, but strangers to the neighbourhood. I mention this in case you thought that the *Boot and Slipper* was patronised by lady persons with two heads.) They got halfway to the bar when one said, 'Ooh, it's a bit *sordid* in here. Let's go in the Saloon Bar.' Which they did.

Arthur, the landlord of the *Boot*, had definite views about the situation. 'They were all right,' he said, 'until they noticed you stood standing there, ponging like an old kipper box. You must admit that you are something only a mother could love. Why do you do it?'

'Why do I do *what*?' I asked, thinking that perhaps Arthur was verging on the personal.

'Go fishing.'

'Why does anybody go fishing?'

'I'm asking you.'

'I'd have thought it was perfectly obvious. People go fishing to . . . er . . . For . . . er . . . Whereas some of us . . . And on the other hand . . . Dear me – is that the time?'

* * *

Why do I go fishing? Why do any of us? I need to think this through so that next time I'm asked, I can come up with an answer as quick as a flash. A defiant replication to squash the opposition. Save a lot of time and racking of the old brain.

Let's try the usual reasons first.

I go fishing because I like the open air life.

Not true, even though I am a Sagittarian. Sagittarians are intelligent, lovable, good looking, athletic and fond of the Great Outdoors. I am not fond of the Great Outdoors.

I can't stand all that rain and wind and snow and fog and stuff. When the sun comes out my eyes water and my nose peels. When it goes in I turn a funny blue colour, break out in goose pimples and suffer from severe seizing up of the knees.

I go fishing because I like to commune with Nature.

I talk to the trees, yes. But I prefer to conduct the conversations in my own back garden so that I don't get taken away. I do have the odd chat on the bank with a passing duck, but the duck usually presumes too much on our acquaintance and scoffs the groundbait. At which point I clout it with the landing net, which leaves the duck feeling groggy and me feeling guilty.

Communing with Nature, if you are to do it properly, seems to involve a lot of soppy things such as prancing through fields with a daffodil behind each ear and spouting poetry. I am not in favour of doing soppy things such as these. Somebody might be looking.

I go fishing because I am fond of all God's creatures.

So why aren't all God's creature fond of me? Why do horses bite me and bullocks chase me and dogs mistake me for a lamp post? Why do gnats and wasps and such zoom in to have their wicked way?

If I'm so fond of God's creatures, why do I spend such a lot of time chucking maggots in the water and sticking hooks up their little bums? And though sometimes I chat with a passing duck, I can do this only as kindly Doctor Jekyll. As you have learned from the above, it doesn't take long for Mr Hyde to take over.

I go fishing for relaxation.

All that tramping across fields, climbing over stiles, getting caught in barbed wire in places it's difficult even to talk about, except in a high-pitched voice. That's not relaxation, that's masochism. And all that falling in the water. One of these days I'll catch my death.

If I wanted relaxation, I'd stay in bed.

I go fishing because I am a patient man with a placid temperament.

I am a patient man, but my patience is very soon exhausted.

Every weekend, as do thousands of other dedicated loonies, I get up too early and get back to bed too late. I spend the whole day at the water in a state of chronic impatience and nervous tension, waiting for the float to dip. Which it seldom does.

After an average day (i.e. having caught not a thing), I come home like thousands of other placid fishermen. In a foul temper. Which is soothed by the time honoured methods of beating the wife, playing hell with the kids and kicking the cat.

Patience be buggered.

I go fishing for the company of kindred souls.

That old phoney, Izaak Walton, was responsible for the image of the angler as 'a simple and wise man . . . a quiet man and a follower of peace'. He was partly right.

Simple, I grant you. Simple to the point of idiocy. Just look at the blokes from your own club. Have you ever seen such a bunch of nutters in all your life?

Wise? Crafty, yes. When it comes to fixing the peg draw, cadging bait, fiddling the match results or choosing the likeliest touch for a free pint after the match. But *wise?*

A quiet man? Fish too close to somebody else's swim and listen to his language as he asks you kindly to move elsewhere. Then wash your ears out.

A follower of peace? Now we're really into the fantasy. Count the bodies littering the bank after a disagreement over the weigh-in and try to work out how many are followers of peace.

I go fishing because it's an inexpensive recreation.

Last Season, every fish cost me about eight quid. And if that's inexpensive I'm going to take up backing three-legged donkeys. Come to think of it, I usually do.

* * *

I've been checking on the reasons why other blokes go fishing. None of this gentle, wise, philosophical angler stuff, but the *real* reasons. And it's surprising how many of them are reasons for *not* doing something else, or excuses for doing something other than fishing.

Some blokes, for instance, go fishing because they are homesick. They live at home, but they're sick of it. So every weekend they clear off into the Wild Blue Yonder to live up to their motto: Have Wife, Will Travel.

Then there are the Do-It-Yourself enthusiasts. Every time the wife asks them to do a job around the house they say, 'Do it yourself'.

Their numbers are swollen by the genuine dozy men, the blokes whose idea of bliss is just sitting doing nothing.

It is difficult to sit and do nothing, even in the heart of the countryside, without some public-spirited citizen approaching and asking, 'Why are you sitting there doing nothing?' So fishing is the answer for these lads. They're the ones who choose a sunny and unproductive swim close to the pub, who don't bother to change the bait, and sometimes don't even bother to put the bait on in the first place. Because there is a rod as visible evidence of activity, nobody asks them what they're doing.

There are the unprincipled lads who use fishing merely as a cover, and who often never get near the water. What other activity allows you to clear off for a whole day, or a whole weekend, to an unspecified destination, with no questions asked? Card schools, strip shows, dog tracks, boozers; they all have their quota of devotees who are supposed to be staring at a float.

Then there are the lads who go night fishing in tents, and never stir out of the tents because it's much more interesting in there. Night fishing is a wonderful excuse for their real hobby. 'Fancy a bit of night fishing, darlin'?' sounds much more innocuous than, 'Fancy a bit?'

Finally, there are the lads who go fishing instead of joining the Foreign Legion. They have had some great tragedy in their lives: an unhappy love affair, a financial disaster, missing the Treble Chance by one point, having the wife's mother come to live with them. They can throw themselves into the Noble Art and forget all their troubles. Except the Irish lad who keeps saying, 'How can I forget a girl with a name like Siobhan Maria Concepta O'Hooligan?'

* * *

That's it. I've just realised why I go fishing – to forget.

I'm trying to forget – what was it now?

Hang on. It'll come to me in a minute...

... being extracts from the diaries and other documents of the Sludgethorpe Waltonians. This from the sermon notes of the Rev Eric Little, Vicar of St Cyprian's, Sludgethorpe, and spiritual adviser to the world-renowned angling club.

We are gathered here today...

Dearly Beloved, we are gathered here in such numbers possibly for the last time until next year. There is still another Sunday to go before the onset of the Coarse Fishing Season, but it has been my experience that attendances on such a day tend to fall off in the face of other considerations such as the checking of tackle, cleaning of reels, scouring of maggots and digging of worms.

As always, I have been greatly heartened by the number of weddings between Easter and June, although the intrusion of Lent into the Close Season always poses problems in fitting everybody in. There have been a great number of christenings also, which seems to indicate that what most of you gave up for Lent last year was self-denial.

For a number of years now it has been my duty - nay, my pleasure - to act as unofficial padre to the Sludgethorpe Waltonians. I think my length of service entitles me to make a few observations on the *modus operandi* of the club and the conduct of the members, many of whose faces I do not expect to see again - apart from at the Christmas carol service - for another nine months.

Among the texts I had chosen for today was 'Love Thy Neighbour', and I think I shall start with that. Another was 'Cast Thy Bread Upon The Waters', but all the signs are that cheese will be a better bet for the coming season.

Love thy neighbour. And who is thy neighbour? He could well be a member of the Slagville Piscatorials, in spite of the unChristian feeling generated at the needle match which marred the close of last Season.

It is *not* Christian charity to lob weighted pieces of soap or punctured shampoo sachets – especially medicated ones – into thy neighbour's swim. Nor to cut holes in his keep net while his attention is distracted during the peg draw. It matters not what thy neighbour has done unto you, such as trapping the right elbow of the Waltonians' ace matchman in the counter flap of the *Bricklayer's Arms* on the night before the contest, or putting curry powder in the bran sold to your members as groundbait.

I am, as you know, deeply concerned with the physical as well as the spiritual welfare of my flock, and am always willing to offer prayers for the sick. I do draw the line, however, at making a special intercession for the speedy return to flexibility of Mr Chalky White's casting arm.

And when I preached to you last year that I would make you fishers of men, I did not mean that you could with impunity throw the opposition match secretary in the canal.

Last Season I was touched by the simple faith of one or two of you in the spiritual properties of the water in the font. But once and for all I must stress that it is not holy water, and will not make the slightest difference to the attraction of any groundbait. If you want that kind of thing you must cross the denominational boundaries and try St Malachy's down the road. At least four christenings here have been ruined by the father of the child dipping a can into the font to take the water home with him.

The financial resources of our little church have never been vast, and I was deeply moved during the last few weeks to have so many volunteers from the Waltonians to help maintain the grounds, dig over the flowerbeds, and assist our Sexton with the sad duty of digging the graves.

I was not at all pleased, however, to discover that each volunteer took a bait tin with him and was more interested in collecting worms than the actual task in hand. Especially when I heard one member attempting to bribe another for a grave-digging shift on the grounds that the worms were better fed – and I quote – 'in the boneyard'.

Suffer little children to come unto me. And I mean that most sincerely. For at least twelve weddings last Season I was without a choir because the choirboys were encouraged to cheer on the

Waltonians at their home matches. Not only that, they were encouraged to hinder and obstruct and abuse the opposition – especially when that opposition happened to be Slagville Piscatorials.

The proximity of the canal to the church – as you know, it runs directly behind the social centre which is used by the Mothers' Union, the Sewing Bee and the Brownies – has also posed some problems. During the spell of warm weather last summer, the windows of the hut had to be left open. And some of the language which drifted in on the breeze during the evening matches left a lot to be desired. I could not detect any references to Gomorrah, but there were certainly many to Sodom.

It was particularly embarrassing to the Mother's Union, some members of which were in the process of complaining about the language when they recognised the voices of their husbands among the offenders. This led to some domestic friction and at least three cases of husband battering.

Which brings me to Animal Sunday. As you know, this is an occasion when members of the congregation bring in their family pets for a blessing. It is meant to give us a deeper insight into the wonders of creation, and to thank all dumb creatures for the joy they give us. Despite the most persuasive arguments, I still absolutely refuse to give my blessing to tins of lobs, specials, casters or gozzers, no matter what match result hinges on their performance.

At the close of this little address, we shall be making the usual collection. I say this in the hope that the collection will *not* be quite the usual . . . I mean that this time I should like it to be in money, and English money if at all possible.

Although I appreciate IOUs, even when some of them are signed with such obvious pseudonyms as Napoleon Bonaparte and Mary Whitehouse, and accept ante-post betting slips as an act of faith, I must protest about the number of bottle tops, fruit machine tokens and obsolete raffle tickets which are finding their way into the collection plate.

Foreign currency is another problem. Irish pennies we can get away with. Francs, Deutschmarks or even pesetas are negotiable, providing we get enough of them. But zlotys, roubles, kopecks,

drachmas, Monopoly money and Confederate dollars do not make much impression on the Dry Rot and Spire Restoration fund.

I did think at one time of complaining about the number of Sludgethorpe Waltonian badges I found in the plate, but not any more. I can swap ten of them for one Slagville Piscatorials badge, for which I can realise 30p on the secondhand market.

Brethren, I digress. Should I not see most of you next Sunday, may I wish you all the very best of fishing until next March. In the matches with Slagville, may the best team win. But don't take it too hard.

Will you all rise now and join in the singing of *Say Not The Struggle Nought Availeth*?

What every young girl should know

I was sitting in this pub in Betws-y-Coed. And why not? Somebody's got to sit in pubs in Betws-y-Coed. I couldn't help overhearing the conversation of the young couple at the next table, because I was listening.

She was obviously very keen on him. He was obviously very keen on fishing. So she was trying to impress him with her knowledge of the game.

'That wheel thing on a fishing rod,' she said. 'That's the thing you turn to wind the string in, isn't it?'

Her swain turned a funny colour and staggered off to the bar for a pint of anaesthetic. Love's Young Dream had definitely flown right out of the window.

So gather round, little darlings, if you don't want it to happen to you. Uncle Clifford will tell you What Every Young Girl Should Know about angling.

The first thing a well brought up girl should do on meeting an angler is to turn smartly around and run like hell. Have nowt to do with him, love.

You will ignore this advice because the average angler tends to be devilish handsome, sophisticated, witty, well dressed and generally irresistible. (I could be wrong. Perhaps they're not all like me.) But later on, when you're left at home with the kids, the washing, the gardening and the decorating, you'll be sorry. Don't say I didn't warn you.

The second thing to do, having met the angler and ignored the foregoing advice, is to say as little as possible. Make admiring noises such as, 'Ooh', 'Aah', 'Really?', 'Magnificent!', 'Fantastic!'. Vary it with 'Way out!', 'Too much!', 'Ace!', 'Brill!', or whatever admiring exclamations happen to be in at the time.

It's amazing how little you really have to say, but it's all you need. If you made any constructive comment, you wouldn't be thanked for it. You'd just be interrupting.

If by a rare chance he should ask your opinion on some finer point of the game – such as, 'What would *you* have done with the gudgeon so close to the bank and the landing net at the cleaners?' –

just gasp in awe and say, 'I really couldn't have coped. But I know that *you* would have handled the situation brilliantly.' Then he's off again for another half hour, telling you just how brilliantly he handled it.

It is well worth-while doing your homework on the actual equipment and mechanics of fishing. This saves your putting your foot in it like the girl in the pub. It also gives you some kind of clue to what he's rabbiting on about.

Start with the *rod*. This is the thing he wags about on the bank and it's usually made up of three pieces. The top joint connects to the middle joint and the middle joint connects to the butt joint.

Got it?

De top joint connekka to de middle joint.
De middle joint connekka to de butt joint.
Now hear de word of de Lawd...

Sorry about that. I get carried away sometimes.

The *line* – not, for Pete's sake, the *string* – runs through *rings* attached to the rod thing. One end of the line, the bit he chucks in the water, is attached to the *hook*. The hook is the thing which misses the fish's mouth when he strikes. Or comes off if it doesn't miss.

The *strike* is the action of lifting the rod to hook the fish. It is usually made about three seconds too late or three seconds too early.

A few inches, or feet, above the hook is the *float*. This is the thing which bobs up and down in the water when the fish takes the bait, and which enables the angler to strike three seconds too late or three seconds too early.

The *bait* is usually something revolting such as a maggot, worm, bits of old cheese or long-dead sausage. Whatever it is, it will eventually put a strain on your marriage, assuming that events would ever lead up to such a situation.

The other end of the line from the hook is attached to the *reel*, which is the windy-up thing at the blunt end of the rod. The reel is used for making tangles of the line when the angler casts out and reels in. Now and again it falls out of its sockets and drops in damp sand, which does wonders for its interior mechanism. This damp sand is something he should clear out immediately or, failing that, at the end of the Season. He never does. This causes him to write angry letters to the reel manufacturers, providing the guarantee hasn't run out.

The *landing net* is a net used for landing fish which are stuck on the hook thing at the end of the line. It is carried in two halves, the net and the handle. The idea is to join the two halves together before the angler starts fishing, and to keep it by his side for instant use. He seldom does this, and at the first cast hooks a whopper and loses it. If he does make up the net beforehand, he leaves it at the top of the bank and can't reach it when the float goes *whump*!

The *keep net* is staked out in the water, in a gentle current and a shady position. This keeps the beer beautifully cool. Now and again the angler puts a fish into the net. The fish cruises around for two or three minutes to get its breath back, then swims out through the holes in the mesh.

The *basket* is made of wicker and is used for holding things and sitting on. Sitting on it for any length of time imprints the reverse image of the wicker on the subcutaneous fat covering the angler's gluteal muscles. This condition is known in medical circles as Basket Bum, and though aesthetically undesirable, is neither serious nor catching. It should be no business of yours, anyway, until you come to know him better. If at that stage of your relationship the sight proves too much to bear, you can always treat the affected area with a hot steam iron applied through a sheet of brown paper. If you get fed up with ironing every weekend, buy him a stool.

The *tent* is another piece of equipment the use of which you will discover as your relationship progresses. He uses it mainly for night fishing. He says. If you go night fishing with him, you will discover what he uses it for.

The *reel oil* is kept in a container which looks suspiciously like a Scotch bottle. This is because it *is* a Scotch bottle, the traditional receptacle for reel oil. He will use about half a bottle every trip.

The contents of the bottle may look like Scotch, smell like Scotch, taste like Scotch. But if he says it's reel oil, it's reel oil. Believe him. The only alternative is to start off your relationship on a basis of mistrust. You wouldn't want that, would you? After all, he's got an honest face.

But don't say I didn't warn you.

On the trail of the hairy bottle

Tony, mate of Cousin Jim from Leeds, had a horror story to tell.

At the back end of the Season, Tony's lad James was left with half a tin of maggots. Tony got the job of disposal, as tends to happen to dads, and buried them two feet down in the garden.

A couple of weeks later he was idly prodding the flowerbed at the burial spot when *Things* started to appear.

'Big hairy things,' said Tony. 'With wings.'

'Bluebottles?' I asked.

'I dunno,' he said. 'It *was* the spot where I'd buried the maggots, but these things had fur coats on. And the *size* of them! Frightened the life out of me.'

Giant hairy bottles? Emerging to terrorise Leeds and its environs? Eek! Were they some kind of super-strain, developed after years of selective breeding on maggot farms? This was a case for Sherlock Parker.

'One thing, Tony,' I said, 'before I start making an idiot of myself. Where had you been before you saw the bottles?'

'Oh. Ah. Er . . . the *Prospect*.'

'And what's the brew?'

'Tetleys. You get a lovely drop at the Prossy – but that had nowt to do with it,' said Tony, ignoring the old-fashioned look from June, his Ever Loving. 'As true as I'm standing here, they had fur coats on.'

So I took up the case. The Quest for the Hairy Bottle. Knowing, even as I did so, that my reputation as a sober and upright pillar of angling society could well be at stake.

First I rang Mel Russ, Features Editor of that excellent journal *Angler's Mail*, and asked, 'Are commercially-bred bluebottles bigger and hairier than ordinary bottles?'

'I worry about you sometimes,' said Mel.

Nothing daunted, or not very much daunted, I rang up a maggot breeder. He'd be bound to take the question seriously and would possibly be eager to claim the biggest and hairiest bottles in the world.

His answer was brief and to the point, though not all that illuminating.

'Don't ask me no silly bloody questions,' he said. 'My game's bloody fishing, not acting bloody daft.'

Thanks a bunch. If there's ever anything I can do for you...

By now severely daunted, but determined to crack the case, I telephoned another breeder: Don Savage at his Yorkshire Maggot Farms near Doncaster. His were almost certainly the maggots which had been buried in Leeds. Why hadn't I thought of that before?

'Yerss...' said Don, thoughtfully. 'And where had your mate been before he saw the hairy bluebottles?'

'The *Prospect,*' I said. 'In Leeds.'

'I see. And what's the brew?'

'Tetleys.'

'That could explain a lot.'

'No, seriously,' I said, 'are your breeding bottles bigger and hairier than the common-or-garden ones?'

'They're bigger,' said Don, 'on account of being bred like racehorses. And very muscular. But not hairier. They're impeccably well-dressed and clean-shaven. All with *bona fide* pedigrees. And if your mate had looked more closely, he would have known if they were ours.'

At last we were getting somewhere.

'How?' I asked.

'We stamp the pedigree on them,' he said. 'Each one has a little brand on its backside.'

Have you ever had that feeling? But Don hadn't finished yet.

'And he would certainly have recognised the ones we feed on poultry – they're covered in feathers.'

Touché. Which is French for I walked straight into that. Still, it was good for a laff, which is more than you could say for t'other feller. But the investigation had got no forrarder.

The Natural History Museum in London: that was the answer. They'd be bound to know, and they're used to dealing with daft questions from anglers.

'Did it happen during mild weather?' asked the sympathetic lady person, expert on all sorts of creepy-crawlies, who answered the phone.

'Yes,' I said. 'Come to think of it. That long cold spell had just ended.'

'Solitary bees,' she said. 'They winter underground and emerge with the warmer weather. Some of them are quite big. They're black. And they're very hairy.'

Got it! At last. Must ring Tony and tell him the news. Stop him fretting.

June, his Ever Loving, answered the phone.

'That's a relief,' she said. 'Give me solitary bees any day. I'll tell Tony when he comes in, though I'm not sure he'll be so pleased.'

'No? Where is he, then?'

'Down at the *Prospect*. Telling stories about giant hairy bluebottles...'

Hands off his outfit

The back end of March and the front end of April see a large number of angling marriages; not so much on account of the Budget as on account of the fact that the Coarse Season is over for a bit and the lads can spare the time to do the things a man's got to do. If they can't get out of it, that is.

The back end of April, any given time in May, and the first two weeks in June see the end of some of these same marriages. The honeymoon is over. After the first, fine, careless rapture, the young brides come face to face with the realities of conjugal bliss with an angler.

The approach of the new Season in June is the real danger time, the time when love may fly out of the window and the short-lived alliance end in a storm of recrimination, castigation, thick ears and missing teeth. Things usually go wrong when the young bride gets hold of and gives away, tubs or destroys her Ever Loving's fishing Outfit.

The Outfit, unbeknownst to her, has been with him for many years, and has come to mean more than a woman ever could. It has protected him against hail, rain, snow, fog, frost, intermittent sunshine and Force Nine gales in exposed areas.

Allowing for a few variations caused by individual taste and the dictates of fashion, the Outfit consists of some basic and venerable bits of protective or decorative clothing. Gather round, girls, and Uncle Clifford will tell you all about it so that you, at least, can avoid putting your marriage at risk.

Starting from the top, and working down to the naughty bits, a typical outfit comprises:

The headgear. This can be a woollen bobbly hat, a camouflaged bush hat, a Castro-type peaked cap, a Japanese kamikaze job that buttons under the chin and makes the wearer look a right idiot, a John West salmon tin sou'wester or a trouble-at-mill flat 'at. It is often difficult to tell which kind it is because of the half-hundredweight of badges pinned all over it.

The gansey. This is a pullover as full of holes as a cheese grater, with every other row of stitches unravelled and hanging down like permed spaghetti. It is usually of such enormous antiquity that the British Museum could well display it among the Ancient English Artefacts.

The anorak is the cause of much of the marital discord, not so much because of its intrinsic yuckiness as for what is crammed in the pockets. Do not, under any circumstances and whatever the temptation, so much as look in the pockets, let alone remove anything you may find festering there. (You can learn all about the horrors awaiting you in the later chapter: 'Pick a Peck of Pickled Pockets'.)

The long johns. After a hard winter and a harder spring, the long johns are often the most revolting spectacle a bride is called upon to face. Until she gets to:

The lucky socks. Like all men called upon to brave the elements and do battle with the forces of Nature, anglers are very, very superstitious. Articles of clothing worn during a Great Victory tend to be treasured unwashed for the rest of eternity. Which is why lucky socks of any long standing do not find much appeal in female eyes, especially if they are family heirlooms such as the lucky socks once belonging to the loved one's grandad and passed on after a further twenty years' use by the loved one's father. With never a drop of soap and water to break the run of luck since the Peterloo Massacre.

The trousers. Hard wearing, functional, virtually indestructible. They have been worn very hard over hill and dale, over stile and barbed wire, through public and saloon bars. Surviving repeated soakings, freezings and rippings for more years than enough. The wicker pattern impressed onto the seat of the pants from long hours on the basket is carved in high relief in a quarter-inch thick coating of dried cow muck, the result of a thousand flips into a thousand flops, inseparable from the approach to the water on a thousand misty dawns.

The footwear. Sometimes a pair of ex-army gravel crushers, sometimes a pair of kinky shooting boots or a pair of bloodstained and teeth-pitted Doc Marten's. But mostly a pair of beat-up and perished old wellies, patched with a puncture outfit or strips of old bicycle inner tube. The wellies are never ever waterproof, because that would defeat their function, which is to let in enough water to warn the angler when things are getting damp underfoot.

Right, girls. Now you know what it's all about. You're ready for Uncle Clifford's Five-Point Plan for Marital Survival.

1. If you don't know where he's put his Outfit, don't look for it. You don't know how lucky you are.

2. If there is a smell in the wardrobe, in the attic, under the stairs or in the shed, that's likely to be it: a ripe and revered Outfit laid carefully to rest in a heapled crump until the start of the new Season. Unless it's actually moving, don't touch it. Some Outfits, grasped by unskilled hands, or hauled out of hiding on pitchforks or between fire-tongs, have been known to crumble into dust.

3. If you do bring the Outfit into the light of day and it survives, don't try to give it away to a passing tramp. He's done you no harm. Most tramps of taste and discrimination, anyway, would not touch an angling Outfit if it were given away with Green Stamps and a bottle of Scotch.

Should you find a tramp daft enough to take it, he would be back within a few days, waving a writ for personal damage and loss of privacy and hygiene. Many a tramp has been bitten by things lurking in the long johns, and more than one has been bitten by the long johns themselves.

4. Don't try and give the Outfit to the local jumble sale, or deserving organisations such as Oxfam. In the first instance you may be landed with a bill for fumigating the parish hall. In the second, there may be a polite note from Oxfam, thanking you kindly but pointing out that they were never that desperate.

5. Don't put it in the washer. The long johns and lucky socks disintegrate into a grey sludge which clogs the pipe when you try to drain the water off. The gansey shrinks to a cross between a Dead Sea Scroll and a pickled walnut. The anorak holds up best, but only by virtue of the over-stuffed pockets.

After such a tubbing, the contents of the pockets would be ruined beyond recall, and your Ever Loving would not thank you for that. He might even go so far as to express his disapproval by breaking something large and solid, such as your mother, over your pretty little head.

* * *

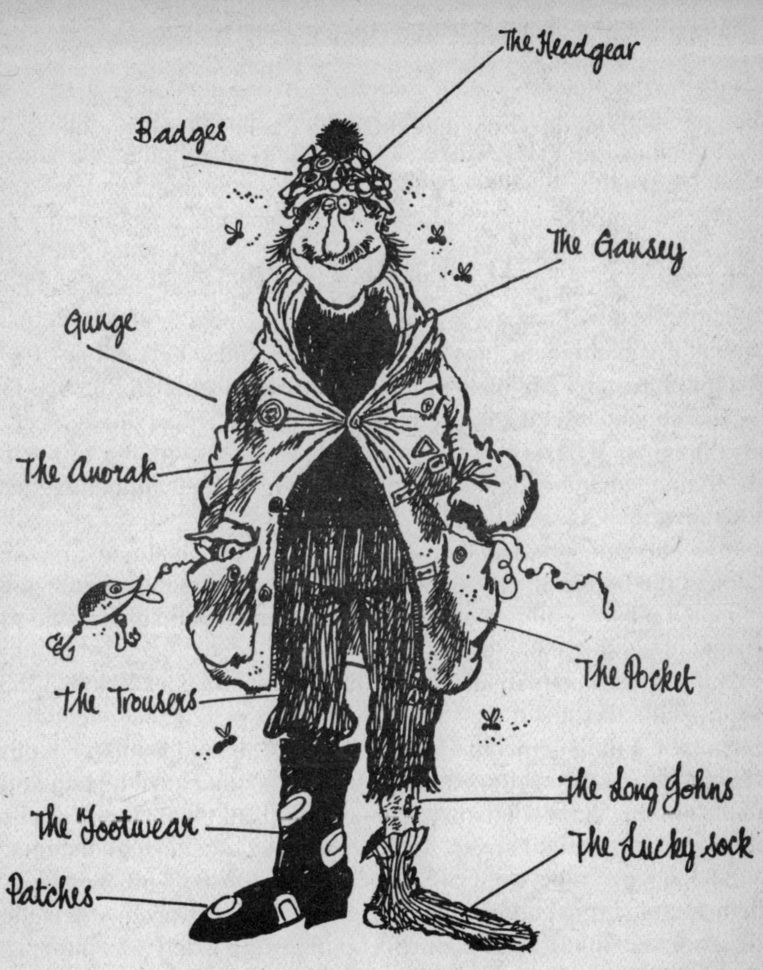

To sum up, what can you do about the Abominable Outfit, ponging away *in situ* until the early summer? In short, and if you know what's best for you, nowt. Wait until you've been married a few years and have got the measure of the lad a bit more. If by that time you know your Ever Loving as well as most anglers' wives know their hubands, you'll feel confident enough one day to take the Outfit outside and shove it under a passing tram. And you'll make very, very sure that he's wearing it at the time.

... being extracts from the diaries and other documents of the Sludgethorpe Waltonians. This from the diary of Horace Harris, the little quiet feller.

Arfer's big case

It was the excitement over the bream that caused all the bother.

Our chairman, Mr Wilfred Harbottle, had landed this big bream at Jackson's Clay Pit. Not only was it big, but it had only one eye and no fins. Mr Harbottle was convinced it was either a hitherto undiscovered hybrid or a completely new species, and called an Extraordinary General Meeting to discuss it.

The meeting was rowdy, as several members claimed to have caught the fish in the past and had felt so sorry for it that they had chucked it back, rather than do the kindest thing and give it a good clout.

But Mr Harbottle would have none of it. Attitudes like that, he shouted above the din, had slowed down the progress of science for centuries. Finally, incensed by shouts of, 'Silly old duffer!' from Harry Turner, he announced that he would parcel up the fish and send it to the Natural History Museum in London. He swept out of the room in a trail of scales, and the meeting broke up in disorder.

The next day he went on a fortnight's holiday and everybody breathed a sigh of relief. Ten days or so later, however, when the time came round for the monthly social night, there was panic in the club. Mr Harbottle had forgotten to hang the key to the safe on its usual hook behind the committee-room door. And in the safe were the bingo tickets.

Several members tried picking the lock with bits of wire, but the old safe stood firm. Then Harry had a bright idea. He would take the safe down to his brother-in-law's garage, and ask him to cut a hole in the back with his acetylene torch.

'The back's only tin,' he said. 'It won't take a minute. And Bingo Night is more important than this safe.'

I helped Harry to load the safe onto a wheelbarrow and we took it in turns to push it along Foundry Road.

'Hey up,' said Harry, who was pushing at the time. 'Here's trouble. Doxon of Dick Green.'

It was Police Constable Arthur Mow, known of course as Arfer, ace sleuth of the Sludgethorpe Constabulary. He and Harry had known each other since they were lads, and it had always been Arfer's ambition to get Harry on something big.

'And what have we here?' rumbled Arfer, blocking the way of the barrow.

'This,' said Harry, 'is a giraffe with a broken leg which we are taking to be put down.'

'Don't come the funny stuff with me, Turner. What's in that safe?'

'Bingo tickets.'

'I told you not to come the funny stuff. Wheel it to the station and let's have a look. I'll give you bingo tickets, Turner.'

Harry wheeled the barrow into Foundry Road Police Station, an edifice with which he was not unfamiliar.

'Why don't you explain properly?' I whispered.

'Ssh!' said Harry. 'We can save all that traipse round to the brother-in-law's.'

Arfer took a bunch of keys from behind the counter and started trying the lock. The fifth key did it.

'Aha!' cried Arfer, and plunged his hands into the interior. Then, sounding all disappointed, 'These are just flaming bingo tickets!'

'Ten out of ten,' said Harry.

'Wait a minute – there *is* something else here . . .'

Arfer pulled out a brown paper parcel, tied with string. There was a weird, phosphorescent glow about it, and it gave off a strange, metallic smell.

'Right!' said Arfer. 'What's all this, then?'

'I'd put that down if I were you,' said Harry, realisation suddenly dawning.

'Something to hide, eh, Turner? We'll soon have it out in the open.'

It was out much sooner than he thought. Arfer held the parcel to his ear and gave it a vigorous shake. The parcel split open and out spilled the oozing remains of a bream, finless and a fortnight dead. It splashed straight into Arfer's right earhole and then all down his uniform.

'Phew!' said Harry. 'Harbottle must have forgotten to post it. We can't stay here to be corpsed. Arfer's contravening the Geneva Convention.'

He gathered up the bingo tickets and dragged me from the station, leaving Arfer stranded, dripping and ponging. Even the desk sergeant had rushed for sanctuary into the charge room.

'Pity about Arfer,' said Harry, back at the club. 'He once trained as a dog handler so he could get promoted. In the end they promoted the dog.

'Right, then! Eyes down looking! All the twos, dinky doos . . . All the sixes, clicketty-click . . .'

Better off dead

There's nothing like having the strength of the insurance companies around you. Nothing like the feeling of security you get from knowing that your Nearest and Dearest will be taken care of if you pop your clogs prematurely, and that your beer money is safe if you are laid up for a bit.

I was thinking that as I started to read a leaflet for an anglers' insurance policy. For less than the cost of two hooks or half a pint of beer a week, it said, you are safe from all the nasties.

By the time I'd finished reading, I was ready to give up fishing for good. There were nasties listed that I'd never even thought about. And I only took up fishing to keep off the streets.

Under this excellent insurance policy you can collect a weekly sum for temporary total disablement; a lump sum for permanent total disablement or the loss of an eye or limb. There appears to be no bonus if you get both eyes poked out, or come home with both legs cut off and everybody calls you Shorty.

Death benefit is not dealt with on a weekly payments basis, perhaps on account of the difficulty the insured person would find in collecting the money. You collect the same lump sum for being dead as you do for being disabled, which seems like earning it the hard way. It seems strange, too, that you only get as much for being dead as for having your eyes poked out, considering the extra effort you have to put into it.

The really frightening bit is the list of specimen questions on the back of the insurance leaflet. You have to ask yourself:

Who stole my rod?

How did my reel get damaged?

Where did I lose my landing net?

Why am I being sued for legal damages of £70,000?

Who will pay while I am off work with this broken leg?

I had to hire transport to get home. Who will pay for that?

Imagine the scene the morning after, trying to remember what happened!

Who stole my rod?

I thought it was that big feller I saw in the *Knacker's Hammer* after the match. The one with the cauliflower ears and broken nose. His rod was a dead ringer for mine.

Perhaps I should have put the proposition a bit more tactfully instead of threatening to take it from him and shove it, section by section, up his nose.

How did my reel get damaged?

It's coming back to me now. After the big feller had crowned me with a pint pot, broken a couple of chairs across my head and skulldragged me round the Public Bar, he started taking the tackle out of my basket and stamping on it.

Where did I lose my landing net?

I remember coming round as he was stamping on my gear, and fetching him one with the landing net handle. He took it off me, broke it in two, and chucked the lot through the window.

Why am I being sued for legal damages of £70,000?

Good question. It does seem a bit steep. But while I was waiting for the ambulance, the landlord of the pub pointed out that the initial disagreement had developed into a general fracas with all the customers joining in. Except for the courting couple in the corner, who had never been known to join in anything.

It spread to the Saloon Bar, and within ten minutes every table, chair and glass in the place was smashed and the pub was on fire. He was sorry to have to sue, the landlord said, but the brewery would be bound to complain when they saw the mess.

Apart from that, the big feller with the cauliflower ears and broken nose was sueing me for defamation, misrepresentation, slander, mental cruelty and hurting his feelings.

The police were also weighing in with charges of threatening behaviour, attempted grievous bodily harm, breach of the peace and saying naughty words.

Who will pay while I am off work with this broken leg?

The insurance company would have paid, presumably, if I'd only remembered to send in the application form and the two hooks or half pint of beer. Who will pay me while I am off work with the other broken leg, God only knows.

I had to hire transport to get home. Who will pay for that?

As I recall, I didn't exactly hire it. The ambulance was called by a public-spirited citizen who noticed that I had difficulty in remaining upright on account of two broken legs and severe unconsciousness.

When the plaster had set, I was given a lift in a police squad car from the hospital to the local nick, where I had to answer some very personal questions.

After the interview I thumbed a lift on the crossbar of a passing bike: a very painful method of transportation, but at least it was cheap.

* * *

Must be grateful for small mercies, I suppose. I could quite possibly have qualified for the Death Benefit. At least it would have kept the wife quiet. She is not in favour of my coming home with both legs in plaster, six teeth missing, all my gear stamped on, being sued for £70,000 and having to appear in court on Thursday.

Come to think of it, that's the one thing the policy doesn't cover: Marital Disharmony and Assault with a Flat Iron.

Perhaps when I do send in the form I'll ask for extra cover. Perhaps they'll even pay me to stay at home.

Just for the record

I've been looking through the *Guinness Book of Records* to see whether I'm in it yet. (*The Writing Rubbish for 30 Years and Getting Away With It Record.*) Not a mention. Obviously a typographical error or a total lack of taste and no susceptibility to bribery on the part of the editors.

They've got some funny records in that book. Piano smashing, standing on one leg, being buried alive, walking backwards, walking on hands, welly throwing and long-distance spitting.

But it has its omissions, apart from the lack of reference to one of Britain's most talented, distinguished and handsome anglers. The angling section is a bit sparse. Just a straight catalogue of largest and smallest fish caught, record weight lists, casting records and that's yer lot. Nothing to laff at at all.

I am now about to rectify this. There's more to fishing than catching fish, as we failures say, and some of the most interesting records come from the spin-off activities of angling.

Here you are, then, Guinness. They're all yours. No fee. Just send me a season ticket for the brewery.

The Falling in the Water Record. Held by Fred Pighead, of Eccles, who fell into the water 67 times in two hours while attempting to fish from the end of a jetty on a Bridgewater Canal coaling basin. The jetty had been shortened by six feet a couple of days before, but Fred – who had been fishing from it for 30 years – refused to believe it.

The Sitting There Without Catching Anything Record. Twenty -nine years and three months, every weekend and most evenings, by Jim Stupid of Warrington, fishing the sulphuric acid outfall of a local chemical factory. Jim also holds the record for losing most hooks – 2,400,543 – and the most nylon traces – 16 miles, 650 yards and 9 inches of them – because they tended to dissolve as soon as they hit the surface. Jim's bid for the 30-year record was foiled by an attack of double pneumonia after a heavy rainstorm, but as a consolation he was awarded *The Daftest Man in the Cemetery Record.*

The Never Getting Found Out by the Wife Record. Every weekend for twenty-six years, loaded down with fishing gear, Cyril

Crafty of Balsall Heath kissed his wife goodbye. He then lit off into the Wild Blue Yonder to indulge in boozing, gambling and knocking about with women. Not once did he get near the water. His wife only discovered this when the record trophy presentation was reported in the local paper, at which point Cyril qualified for *The Most Missing Teeth in Ten Seconds Record.*

The Getting in Trouble With the Wife Record. Sid Henpecked, of Dunmow, was beaten about the head with a rolling pin every Saturday and Sunday night for 45 years by his Ever Loving. She didn't mind him going fishing, but she did object to his coming home at two in the morning, falling about, singing naughty songs and waking the neighbours.

'You soon get used to being beaten over the head every night,' said Sid. 'But it's a hell of a job trying to buy a size 19⅝ cap.'

The Bailiff Dodging Record. Ebenezer Tighthouse, of Duck's Bottom, never paid for a ticket in 47 years. Present at the awards ceremony was a member of the local Water Authority, and Ebenezer is now asking for 10,478 other offences to be taken into consideration.

The Little Fish Stuffing Record. Herbert Kapok, of Uppingham, stuffed 242 sticklebacks in 3 hours 37 minutes. His prize was a pair of dark glasses and a white stick.

The Big Fish Stuffing Record. Still open. Jonah Reddimix, of Portland, is attempting to stuff a whale shark which was washed up on the beach. He went in there three weeks ago and hasn't come out yet.

The Welly Throwing Record. Twenty feet 7½ inches, by Charlie Chuckchuck, of Wigan. The throw is relatively short because, for the angling record, the welly has to be thrown with an angler inside it. Favourite missile is Wee Willie Tremble, who is 4 feet 11 inches tall and weighs 7 stone 3 pounds. 'I'm getting a bit fed up with this,' he said, interviewed in an intensive care unit.

The Steward Telling-Off Record. Cassius Cocky, of Effingham, takes no nonsense from match stewards, and delights in telling them where to go and what to do with their rule books. He recently told off 74 National stewards in two hours. He will receive the trophy as soon as the stitches are taken out.

The Playing a Fish Record. Still open, after the disqualification of Bert 'Blinkers' Magoo of Longsight, who claimed to have played a fish in the Solent for 48 hours 17 minutes before his line parted. Opponents of the claim pointed out that Mr Magoo had hooked the Isle of Wight ferry.

The Slipping on Cowpats Record. Norman Niffey, of Nuneaton, slipped on cowpats 87 times in 35 minutes in a performance which included seven single, five double, and three triple somersaults. He received the award by proxy because the local Health Authority wouldn't allow him into the hall for the presentation. His social life is now not all it could be, because nobody will speak to him and even his best friends won't tell him.

The Trampled on by Bullocks Record. George Flatt, of Yelling, was trampled on by 56 bullocks in a 15-minute crossing of the pasture from the river bank. He is now as well as can be expected after simultaneous operations in Wards 10, 11 and 12 of Yelling Animal Sanctuary, but is reported to be suffering from a severely split personality.

The Caught on Barbed Wire Record. Fred Lacking, of Bolsover, was snagged 122 times in a 200-metre barbed-wire hurdle. The fame this record has brought him will probably help the sales of his other record – the LP, *Your Favourite Angling Songs by Fred Lacking* (soprano).

The Lie Telling Record. Honest John Whopper, of Washington, told 9.7 fibs a minute for 12 hours 18 minutes while describing his angling successes. He would have gone on longer, but he was struck by lightning.

The Number of Lady Persons in a Nightfisher's Tent Record. Held by Randy Fruit, of Cockfosters, who managed to squeeze 37 consenting females into a standard-sized nightfisher's tent. 'Frustrating,' he said. 'By the time I'd got them all in there wasn't room for me.'

The Number of Polygamous Marriages Record. Held by Gary Glutton, of Ardwick, with 10 wives, one in each Water Authority area of England and Wales. 'Helps me with my match fishing,' says Gary. 'I don't have to worry about making my own sandwiches up. I only hope they don't find out about the Scottish lot.'

* * *

Hang on. While I've been typing this, I've missed opening time at the *Boot and Slipper*. That *is* a record . . .

A clean bill of health

One of the incidents that aroused the wrath of the angling Press was the confiscation at Luton Airport of a fishing team's maggots and casters. It aroused even more wrath than it would normally, because it was a British Press angling team:

MAGGIES IN AIRPORT SHOCK GRAB
CASTERS IN HI-JACK HORROR
AIRLINE BUREAUCRATS SWOOP ON BRITISH BAIT

... that sort of thing.

The team was taking its own bait to Germany for a match with the British Army. Although the maggies and casters were in sealed containers, the airline threw them off the plane. They weren't properly packed, they said. Didn't have a Min. of Ag. health certificate and didn't meet the transit rules of the Min. of Def., who had chartered the plane.

The team had to buy German maggots at the other end and lost the match. To make things worse, the German Customs said they'd have let the British bait in anyway. These days, any maggies of ours are maggies of theirs. But despite the enlightened German attitude, the obstacles at British airports remain.

How *do* you get a Min. of Ag. health certificate, though? Surely it takes days to give a medical to a gallon of maggies. Can you imagine the state of the maggie doctor at the end of the surgery, worn out by saying, 'Say ninety-nine. Bend over. Cough!', ten thousand times?

What could the maggies be suffering from that would result in their being turned down for active service? Flat feet? Halitosis? Colour blindness? Anatto fever? Pinkie rot?

And what happens to the failures? Are they given a week's sick leave, with a diet of fillet steak and best butter? Or are they shunted along the bench to where a maggie disposal operative awaits them with a two-pound hammer?

Even more puzzling are the Min. of Def. transit rules. What must the maggies do to conform? Are they paraded, drilled and inspected before the flight?

'Maggies! Maggies . . . shun! By the right . . . Right . . . dress! Up a bit, Number Seven . . . you 'orrible little gozzer, you! Straighten up Number Four . . . You're not in your bran and milk now, laddie! Eyes . . . front! Stand at – wait for it, *wait* for it . . .'

To avoid all this, it would be much easier to practise some small deception and take the bait on board as hand luggage. But do make sure it's properly packed. My old dad didn't.

He was on a plane trip to fish in France and, knowing that French maggies are scraggy and expensive, he was taking his own. During the flight they made their way out of the parcel which he'd stowed in the overhead luggage compartment. A few started falling onto the young lady person sitting next to him. Then the whole lot came down, doodly-splat into her hair, down her cleavage and all over her nice new dress.

If she'd kept her cool and gently scooped them up – or let the old feller do it – there'd have been no harm done. But she screamed and started swatting at them, smearing them all over her dress. As they were highly coloured in choice fluorescent shades, they made a hell of a mess.

It cost the old man a new dress (for her), several large brandies (for him), a new can of maggies at inflated French prices, and the threat of a lawsuit. As it was, he had his name put in the airline's Naughty Book as a maggie smuggler and upsetter of little darlings.

* * *

While we're on the subject of packing, it would be appropriate to warn anybody who buys maggots in a paper bag never to put them on bar counters. That's how I was once able to track down Mad Mac.

He had rung up and said, 'See you in the *Red Lion*, ol' buddy. Over and out.' And put the phone down.

There were four Red Lions in the area. At the first two I had no luck, but at the third I found the landlord brushing up some wiggly things from the carpet.

'Mad Mac?' I asked.

'Mad Mac,' said the landlord. 'Walking disaster area, he is.'

'Where is he?'

'Left about ten minutes ago. Realised you might be in one of the other *Red Lions*, picked up his paper bag and rushed out.'

'Which other *Red Lion* did he go to?'

'Search me. But the corner of his paper bag had got soggy on the counter and it burst as he left. Just follow the trail.'

Easy peasy. Normally a trail of live maggies doesn't last long, on account of them shifting so fast. But one laid through a busy shopping area, where the poor old things get stepped on, can't be missed. You just follow the spludges.

* * *

A similar, but more spectacular, fate overtook the maggies bought by Tactful Tetters. He didn't have a bait tin with him, and took them away in a paper bag.

On the way home he stopped for a pint, and put the bag on the bar. In walked a big bloke who didn't get served for about five minutes. Finally he lost his patience.

'Is nobody serving in this flaming pub?' he bellowed. And brought the flat of his giant hand crashing down on the counter. Or would have done if the paper bag hadn't been in the way.

Tetters was left with a soggy mess and told by the barman (they're never there when you need 'em) to take it elsewhere.

'I bet you called the big feller some names,' I said, knowing Tetters's way with words and habit of calling a spade a bloody shovel.

'Not really,' said Tetters. 'What can you call a six-foot-four, seventeen-stone bloke who has just squashed your maggies - except "Sir"?'

The Sludgethorpe Diaries

... being extracts from the diaries and other documents of the Sludgethorpe Waltonians. This from the diary of Horace Harris, the little quiet feller.

The day of all flesh

You'd never recognise Jackson's Clay Pit now. There's not a bit of rubbish on any of the banks, not an old pram, bike, bedstead or scrap of paper to be seen. There are no bottles or tins floating on the water. There are no weeded-up swims, no bits which are too overhung to fish, no unsafe bits of undercut bank. And it's all thanks to Harry Turner.

The club Committee has been trying for years to get the pit cleaned up. It's not much of a water, but it's the best we've got so near at hand. Members have always had some excuse for not turning out to help. The Veterans couldn't because of their lumbago, rheumatics, bad legs, bad backs, bad fronts, bad everythings. The Juniors couldn't because of their homework, running errands, doing a paper round. With the able-bodied Senior members it was pressure of work, decorating, gardening, taking the wife to visit her mother.

Then Harry read a story in the paper. An angling club was complaining that women were bathing nude in its waters.

'I've got it,' he said, and wrote a letter to the *Sludgethorpe Echo*. It read:

> Sir,
>
> I wish to complain most strongly about the disgraceful and disgusting state of affairs at one of Sludgethorpe's recreational waters. For several weeks now I have observed young ladies – if they can be flattered by such a term – cavorting in the water in a state of total undress.

Their activities are not confined just to the water. Scarcely a square foot of bank or undergrowth escapes the tread of a naked foot as these persons leap from tussock to tussock in a frenzy of abandonment.

It is time the council or the local constabulary clamped down on this sort of thing. A situation in which respectable anglers or boaters cannot follow their pursuits without their sensibilities being affronted by blatant female nudity cannot - nay, must not - be tolerated.

Disgusted
Foundry Road

The *Echo* comes out on Friday morning. On Friday night the clubhouse was besieged by members, from striplings to old lads on two sticks, who had been overcome by a sudden urge to Keep Sludgethorpe Tidy, to restore the clay pit to its natural beauty, to help enhance the well-earned enjoyment of their fellow men.

On Saturday morning there was no hanging about waiting for the crack of dawn. Before the first sparrow coughed, the place was crawling with public-spirited volunteers. And it crawled until well after dark on Sunday.

'Nice one, Harry,' I said on Monday night, watching from the *Bricklayer's Arms* the file of members climbing down into the pit to carry on the good work. 'But they're bound to tumble to it before long. And if they find out it was you who wrote the letter about the pit, you'll be in real bother.'

'What letter about the pit?' said Harry. 'I didn't once mention the pit. It's not the only water in Sludgethorpe. What about the canal? And the flash behind Sludgethorpe Plastics?'

'Brilliant,' I said. 'Absolutely brilliant.'

We chatted until almost closing time, when in staggered Chalky White, the club's ace matchman.

'Large Scotch,' he croaked. 'What are you two having?'

This was unusual. Chalky is notorious for having the longest pockets and shortest arms in the club.

Chalky's Scotch went down in one. Harry and I thanked him kindly and took the froth off our pints.

'Phwarh!' said Chalky. 'You've missed it. Down there. Seen nowt like it in my life.'

'What?' said Harry.

'All those women. In the nuddy. Starkers. Not a stitch. Splashing around and running about all over the pit. That bloke who wrote to the *Echo* was right. Dozens of 'em!'

It turned out to have been some kind of women's rights organisation who had read the letter and decided to demonstrate their solidarity with their Sludgethorpe sisters. If women wanted to swim starkers, they would swim starkers. And they came down in coachloads to prove it.

That was no consolation to Harry as Chalky dribbled out the news. He grabbed hold of Chalky's lapels and lifted him clear of the floor.

'And you *looked*!' he yelled. 'Like a bunch of bloody Peeping Toms! You stood and gawped! And leered! And drooled! I'm ashamed of you. And everybody else who was down there. A disgrace to the club, the lot of you!'

He put Chalky down.

'I suppose,' he said bitterly, 'the fact that you're here means they've all gone home...'

The rime of the ancient angler

It is an ancient Angler,
And he stoppeth one of three.
'Ah'll tell yer,' he says, 'a hilarious joke
'If a pint yer'll buy for me.'

'Hold off! Unhand me, thou boozy old twit!'
The wedding guest replied.
'Because if you don't, I'll fetch you one.
'Now kindly step aside . . .'

* * *

Sorry, folks. I've been re-writing *The Rime of the Ancient Mariner.* Remember him? He was the old lad with the albatross round his neck who messed up a wedding for one of the guests by telling him a long and unlikely story.

I was reminded of the poem twice recently, first of all by Mad Mac's unwitting evening at a wedding reception. He'd left his tackle on the bank and wandered into a pub. The *Jolly Fisherman,* it was called, and so seemed highly appropriate.

Izaak Walton Bar Upstairs, said a notice. So Mac, thinking he'd pay some kind of homage to the lad, went upstairs. The bar was crowded, and he had to shove his way through to order a pint.

'Paid for,' said the barman, when Mac proffered the money.

Mac peered around the dimly lit bar to see which kind soul had paid for his booze, but everybody was happily chatting in little groups.

'Must be some sort of publicity stunt,' he thought, and spent a jolly couple of hours supping for free and having the odd natter here and there.

His evening came to an end when he chatted up a large and matronly lady person.

'Are you a friend of the bride or the groom?' she asked.

'Ulp!' said Mac, choking on his pint.

Then she looked down and saw his wellies. Not quite *de rigeur* as footwear for the celebration of upmarket nuptials.

'Do excuse me,' said Mac. 'My carriage awaits.'

* * *

... I was reminded of the poem again the other night when I was cornered in a pub by one of those blokes who insist on telling you fishing jokes from the moment they find out you're an angler.

'Sit down,' he said. 'You'll enjoy this.'

'Heard it,' I said. 'Boring. *Boring*...'

'Not *it*,' he said. '*Them*. See if you can spot these puns.'

And then he started. I'm going to repeat them, because I don't see why you shouldn't suffer as well. And at least you'll be forewarned. If you should bump into him after this, he won't be able to get one over. I've put the puns in capital letters to save you the bother of recognising them by their intrinsic brilliance. Boring. *Boring*...

'I don't wish to encROACH on your privacy,' he said. 'But I'll just PERCH on this stool and have a pint. I'm HOOKED on this stuff, you know. I can SINKERnuff to FLOAT a battleship.

'It might sound as if I'm WHALEing, but I don't do it on PORPOISE. If you think I'm shooting a LINE, take me to your LEADER. It's the wife, you see. She's a real old TROUT. Always CARPing.

'The wife said, POUTING, that if I didn't give fishing a REST I'd be making a ROD for my own back. It all started when we went on holiday to Cheddar. We saw lots of gorges. You know, DISGORGE and dat gorge.

'We met a Scotsman with a salmon. I told him to stick it up his KELT. "Do all Scotsmen go salmon fishing?" asked the wife. "Depends," I said. "SALMON 'em do and SALMON 'em don't."

'When I came into this pub tonight, I thought the outlook was BLEAK. It was really RUFFE outside. But the barmaid gave me a BREAMing smile, and I thought, "What a lovely RUDDy complexion, even though she is a bit CHUBby. It's an EEL wind..."

'I know you from somewhere, but I can't quite PLAICE you. Without wishing to SKATE around the problem, didn't I see you somewhere dancing the CONGER?

'A lot of people try to COD me, expecting me to FLOUNDER

about. But 'pon my SOLE, I'm a DAB hand, even though at times I'm hard of HERRING.

'Ah. Is that my pint pot? I'd be grateful if you'd FILLET up. If I'd known you'd be here tonight I would have dressed for the occasion. Perhaps worn my straw BLOATER...'

There was only one way to shut him up, I thought. Fight fire with fire.

'Bet you there are some fish you can't pun on' I said.

'I can see you're a bit FLY,' he replied. 'What's your ANGLE, eh?'

'Come on,' I said. 'See what you can do with these – starting with *Zander.*'

'If I can't phone the wife tonight I'll ZANDER a telegram.'

'*Pike.*'

'The bit I like best about hotpot is the PIKErust on the top.'

'*Barbel.*'

'I like to keep fit by weight training. Nothing like lifting the old BARBELs for getting a bit of weight off. Why, sometimes I'm just a SHADow of my former self. Thought I'd throw that in for free, old son.'

'*Catfish.*'

'Easy. Ever seen a CATFISH for tadpoles?'

'*Haddock.*'

'I HADDOCKoff last week, but I'm better now.'

'*Grayling.*'

'I say, your hair's turning GRAY-LINGer a while and tell me what caused it.'

This time, I thought, I've got to nail him. Ah-ha!

'*Stickleback.* Get out of that!' I cried, desperately.

'Funny you should mention that,' he said. 'I was out in the car the other day when I stopped to watch a chap fishing. He didn't like being disturbed and came at me waving a damn great stick. "Look here, old son," I said. "If you don't put down that STICKLEBACK right over your tackle with my car." Get it?'

I left the pub with his voice still ringing in my ears: 'I say, old son, have I dropped some kind of POLLACK?'

And I recalled how the wedding guest made his exit from the Ancient Mariner:

He went like one that hath been stunned,
And is of sense forlorn:
A sadder and a wiser man,
He rose the morrow morn...

Dressing to kill

We were walking by the river: Dearly Beloved and I and a respectable (i.e. non-angling) married couple. From further along the bank came the blast of a whistle.

'Sounds like the end of a fishing match,' said I, making polite conversation. 'Ah, yes. That's the steward with the scales up there.'

'How interesting,' said the respectable wife person, making polite conversation back. But the foreknowledge did not prepare her for the sight which was to come.

Up the bank and into the field lurched fifty of the most desperate looking characters outside of a bad Zapata movie. Stubble-chinned, gap-toothed, dressed in the weirdest assortment of combat suits, camouflage jackets, wellies, waders and flying boots, and each lugging a dripping net.

'Eek!' screamed the respectable wife person. 'What on earth are those?'

'I think the Cubans have landed,' said the respectable husband person. 'Take cover!'

'Have no fear,' I said, fighting down the urge to turn and run. 'They are no more than the stalwart lads who have been fishing this stretch. They're quite harmless really.'

But I knew then what Wellington meant when he looked at the British lot sent over to Spain for an away fixture against Napoleon's 'A' team.

'I don't know what effect these men will have upon the enemy,' said the Iron Duke, 'but, by God, they terrify me.'

* * *

Not that it behoves me to criticise the way other people dress. Recently, Dearly Beloved marched me into a natty gents' outfitters and made me buy a quilted anorak.

Very smart, it was. And warm. The only snag was that it wasn't waterproof. I found out the hard way and came back from the water all soggy and sniffling.

I went straight round to the shop. 'Look at this,' I said. 'One shower of rain and I'm soaked to the skin.'

'Ah,' said the natty gents' outfitter, 'I didn't *say* it was *waterproof*, did I?'

There was no answer to that. Except mayhap a swift application of the right welly to the naughty bits. But that would hardly be the action of a gentleman and a scholar.

So the other day I rescued my old fishing jacket from the garage. Shabby it may be. And a touch crumpled. But waterproof it most definitely is.

'Just a minute, Worzel,' said Dearly Beloved. 'Where do you think you're going in *that*?'

'Fishing,' I said. All steely and determined.

'You are definitely not stirring over the doorstep in that thing,' came the tinkling tones. 'Three tramps and a jumble sale turned it down last week.'

'Now look here –' I said.

'And why are you wearing one white sock and one red one?'

'These are my lucky socks. I've got another pair just like them upstairs. You can't see them once I've got my wellies on, anyway.'

I was allowed out on condition that I wore my new, quilted, water-absorbent anorak where anybody might see me, and packed the old, waterproof, jacket for the bank. And that under no circumstances would I take my wellies off in company. (On that score she needn't have worried: whenever I take my wellies off there is instantly a distinct lack of company.)

* * *

I only wish now that long ago I'd been firmer about the gas cape and the goatskin rug.

The gas cape was a relic of my National Service days, and there was nothing to beat it for all-round insulation. It had a hood with a drawstring so that I could fish with only the end of my nose sticking out. It also had a big hump on the back, so that the army pack could be worn underneath.

The hump served no purpose in civilian life, and had the drawback in winter of collecting snow very quickly. If I sat still for ten minutes I looked just like a snowman, and often had trouble from little lads and wandering dogs: one lot throwing snowballs and the other lot cocking their legs up. The hump had the other drawback, at any time of year, of giving old ladies heart attacks whenever I got on a bus. There's something about a camouflaged Quasimodo that causes palpitations to set in.

The cape was last seen in a monsoon-type rainstorm, draped round a grateful dustman. I bet the mortality rate among old ladies on his round really rocketed after that.

The goatskin rug was getting a bit tatty after ten years in front of the fire. When it was thrown out I salvaged it, cut a hole in the middle for my head, tied a belt round it, and there it was – a warm, waterproof, hairy poncho.

'You can take that off *now*,' said the Light of My Life. 'I've put up with some things in my time, but I'm definitely drawing the line at Hereward the Wake.'

I was upset about that. Rather fancied myself as Hereward the Wake. But apart from sulking for a week, sucking my thumb and refusing to eat my greens, I took it like a man.

I really will have to be firm about the next piece of natty attire. I've always wanted a Davy Crockett hat. Real ones are hard to come by on account of being made of raccoon skin, and there is a definite shortage of raccoons in our neck of the woods.

But I've got my eye on the next best thing, and I shan't have to wait too long. Daft Cat's definitely getting on a bit. Isn't 'oo, Jemima . . . ?

Shock treatment

This car was wobbling on buckled wheels up the road, and bits kept dropping off it. It stopped on the white line, bang in the middle of the road, and the driver got out. He could get out easily because, as soon as the car stopped, the offside door fell off.

The driver stood by the car, traffic whizzing past on either side, saying plaintively, 'Where am I? I think I've had an accident.'

He had, poor lad. Two miles back. In a daze he'd driven on, then realised something had happened, and stopped. As soon as the kindly locals took him in hand, he went to pieces, trembling violently and flopping about all over the place. Delayed shock, that was. It took several brandies to get him on an even keel.

His condition was a classic example of the effect a sudden traumatic experience can have on the nervous system. I mention it to lead up to the fact that the average angler has at least one traumatic experience every outing, and therefore often returns home in a state of delayed shock.

Signs of delayed shock in an angler are an unsteady gait, difficulty in focusing, and a tendency to fall down if left unsupported for any length of time. If more wives, girlfriends and other interested parties would recognise the symptoms, there would be an immediate reduction in the number of battered anglers.

The mere sight of an angry lady person in curlers and dressing gown can induce secondary shock and send the poor lad into a catatonic trance, an easy victim for the coal shovel or whatever means of wifely therapy is about to be applied. Another school of thought has it that such a sight can result in the angler immediately sobering up - sorry, immediately recovering his equilibrium - though such cases are relatively rare.

The traumatic experiences of angling are too many and varied to list more than a few, but the following examples should serve to illustrate the commoner causes of shock:

1. He catches a record pike.
2. He misses a record pike.

3. He catches a pike which is nothing to get excited about, but which bites his finger off.

4. He catches the first decent-sized catfish of his life, which frightens him almost to death. (Analysis of anglers' reactions to such a confrontation – that enormous mouth, those evil little eyes, those horrible waving whiskers – show that the shock to the system is the equivalent of opening the front door and finding the mother-in-law standing on the step.)

5. He catches 300lb of bream and strains himself lifting the keep net.

6. He catches 300 drams of gudgeon (a personal best) and they all swim out through the holes in the net. At the end of the day, intent on showing off his catch, he gives the net a titanic heave. And falls flat on his back.

7. He falls down the bank into ice-cold water. Not so bad if it's soft water, but very painful in hard water areas.

8. He falls down the bank, misses the nasty cold hard water and hits a nice warm rock. Unfortunately, there are no soft rocks.

9. He wins the match for his team and is beaten senseless by thumps on the back.

10. He loses the match for his team and is beaten senseless by thumps all over. Not to mention being perforated by rod rests and having ill-tempered pike stuffed down his trousers by ill-tempered team-mates.

11. He wins the match and is bought drinks all night.

12. He loses the match and has to buy drinks all night.

These examples of just some of the hazards an angler faces will hopefully get him a more sympathetic reception on his return to the old homestead. You must remember, ladies, that an angler in delayed shock is like a sleepwalker: on no account must he be rudely awakened or upset in any way.

An angler's wife or sweetheart, or both, can assume that he almost always will return home in a state of shock, and can prepare his treatment in advance. Get made up, do your hair, and put on something slinky (not that army surplus greatcoat again). Practise welcoming smiles: you know, the ones you gave him when you were courting. Or before he took up fishing.

When you hear a knock, open the front door carefully in case his mates have propped him up and run away. Take him gently by the arm and lead him into the house with loving care and soothing words.

Take his gear from him (don't worry that the keep net is dripping all over the carpet) and sit him in the armchair by the fire. Remove his wellies and replace them with his slippers.

Stroke his fevered brow and whisper things like, 'And did you have a lovely time on the bank today, darling?' Hand him his nightcap: a tumbler of hot milk laced with Scotch (for severe cases, a tumbler of Scotch laced with hot milk).

Of course you must be prepared initially for the treatment itself to bring on secondary shock. It takes some getting used to.

One angler was being very lovingly treated by his spouse when she asked, 'How are you now, darling? Are you enjoying it?'

'I am that,' he said. 'I could stand this all night. But the wife'll kill me when I get home...'

A pain in the psst-psst-psst...

There are some things it is difficult even to talk about. A splinter in the bum is one of them.

I got it from a stile. I was doing the high-kick routine over the top when a sudden gust of wind caught basket, anorak and holdall and threw me off balance. My left buttock, if you'll pardon the indelicacy, slid down the post until its progress was arrested by –

Aaaaarrrrgh!

I may not be a scholar or a gentleman, but I *am* a coward. It hurt, did that. About an inch and a half of seasoned timber. Half an inch sticking out, the other inch stuck well in.

With the true stoicism of our island race I screamed for a bit, then grasped the end of the splinter. Closing my eyes and thinking of England, I gave it a gentle tug. It broke off, leaving the stuck-in bit still stuck in.

I felt carefully down through the layers of thermal underwear to the afflicted spot. There was no timber left outside to get hold of. I was, as they say, stuck with it.

The choice was to go all the way back home and have it seen to by Dearly Beloved, losing a morning's fishing by so doing, or carry on down to the water. As I'd arranged to meet up with Mad Mac and Big McGinty – and as I'd paid for my day ticket – I decided to carry on.

Off I set, my left leg locked stiff to ease the stabs of pain which came every time I bent it. I should have gone home...

'Here he is!' yelled Mad Mac from the bank. 'Hi there, ol' buddy! What's with the Long John Silver bit?'

I waited until I was within whispering distance.

'I've got a splinter,' I hissed.

'Where?' asked Mac.

'Sssh! In my psst-psst-psst...'

'Har!' yelled Mac. 'McGinty! Lissen to this! He's got a splinter in his –'

Mac's breath was cut short by a swift application of thumb to windpipe.

'Don't tell 'em all,' I muttered through clenched fillings.

McGinty lumbered up.

'Wassermarrer?' he panted.

'Psst-psst-psst,' I said.

'Har!' he yelled. 'A splinter in the – euk!'

'Sorry about that,' I said. 'Promise to keep quiet?'

McGinty nodded and I released the dreaded Indian Death Lock.

'Seriously, though,' he said, 'you could get tetanus from a thing like that. Could possibly be fatal. Will you leave me your river rod?'

'Hey, I wanted that,' said Mac.

'I saw this film once,' said McGinty, 'where somebody treated a snake bite by cutting a chunk out of the wound. I could try that if you like.'

'I'm not over-keen,' I said.

'Then he sucked the poison out and – come to think of it, I'm not over-keen either,' said McGinty.

'John Wayne had this hole in him where he'd pulled an arrow out,' said Mac. 'And he poured some gunpowder in and set fire to it. Right as rain in no time.'

'John Wayne was only kidding,' I said. 'And besides which he got paid for it. Would anybody mind if we got some fishing in?'

* * *

By the middle of the morning I was weary from standing up, and the wound had begun to throb.

'By the cringe,' I said to Mac. 'This doesn't half hurt.'

A large and mature lady person walking her dog caught the agonised expression which flitted across the otherwise inscrutable Parker visage.

'You seem to be in pain,' she said. 'Can I help? I'm a trained nurse.'

'Thank you kindly, madam,' I said, kicking Mac in the kneecap as he started to open his mouth. 'But not to worry. It's only my old wound playing up. Does it in the damp weather, you know.'

If Mac had had the splinter, the trained nurse would have been a twenty three year old blonde and beautiful nymphomaniac. What I was offered was merely the Luck of the Parkers.

'What you need, ol' buddy,' said Mac, 'is some warmth and comfort. We'll take you for a pint.'

* * *

'What's up with Cliff?' asked Ben, landlord of the *White Hart*. 'Doesn't seem his usual happy-daft self.'

'He's got a splinter in his psst-psst-psst,' said Mac, before I could stop him.

'Har!' screeched Ben. 'Hear that, lads? Parky's got a splinter in his bum!'

Har har, ho ho, yuk yuk, went the assembled throng.

'That,' I said to Mac, 'will cost you a large one.'

'Pleasure, ol' buddy,' croaked Mac. 'As soon as you let go of me neck.'

* * *

That evening, I presented myself at the surgery of Doc Thumper, physician extraordinary and a dab hand with splinters.

'There it is, our Clifford,' he said, holding up a bloody and gruesome exhibit between tweezers before my watering eyes. 'I'd better give you a tetanus jab, considering where this thing came from. Where would you like it?'

'Pick your spot, Doc,' I said. 'I've already got one pain in the bum.'

'Right,' said Doc. 'Bend over . . .'

I was a sagger maker's bottom knocker for the FBI

I find having my hair cut a painful business psychologically, on account of a childhood experience when a talkative barber did a neat trimming job with a pair of clippers on my left ear.

Since then I have tended not to have my hair cut often. And all I ask of any barber is to watch where he's sticking his clippers and to keep his big yap shut.

Which makes my present tonsorial artiste a bit hard to bear.

Not only does he never shut up. Not only is he an expert on any subject you care to mention, or not to mention. Not only does he fancy himself as a bit of a wag, telling jokes which are worse and older than mine. Not only does he practise, right into my sensitive earhole, the harmonies for his barber shop quartet with which one day he hopes to sweep the streets. Not only all of this – but he is also currently on a health food kick.

It sounds harmless enough, but his particular health food is a mixture of bran, oats and wheat germ, all mixed up in a plastic bucket which he keeps by the basin. Every couple of minutes he scoops up a handful, crams it into his mouth, and carries on talking while he chomps it. Spraying me with a stream of chaff which gets down my neck, in my ears and right up my nose.

'And what do you do for a living, then?' he asked the other day, during my half-yearly all-off. Giving out with the chaff like the reject chute of a combine harvester.

I had had enough.

'I'm a bluebottle sexer on a maggot farm,' I said.

'You're a what?'

'Look, I'm a bit sensitive about my job and I get fed up with people disbelieving me and taking the mickey. So if you don't mind, I'd rather keep quiet and listen to your views on the current world economic situation.'

'No, no,' he said. 'Straight up. I get all sorts in here, you know. Man of the world, me. Some of my best friends, you'd never believe what they do for a living. Tell me about it. What's with the bluebottle sexing?'

'If you insist,' I said, taking a deep breath. 'But hereafter you are not to interrupt.

'Yes, but –' he said.

'Shurrup,' I said. 'First, you must understand that maggot farms are a vital part of our economy, breeding maggots not only for home use by millions of British anglers, but also for export to countries in which the selective breeding techniques have not yet reached the peaks of British sophistication.'

'Oh, yes,' he said. 'I know all about that. Only the other day –'

'And the most important part of this selective breeding is the choice of parents for the maggots. They must be pure-bred bluebottles of impeccable pedigree, giant physique and above average intelligence.'

'How do you – ?'

'Furthermore – and this is where I come in – the balance of the sexes in the breeding cages must be exactly right: one male bottle to every twenty female bottles. Otherwise, as I'm sure you'll appreciate, they would fight to the death for the favours of the female bottles. Nor would it simply be a question of Survival of the Fittest – many of those who survived would be in no fit state to perform that essential office for which Nature has created them. I have to sit right next to the breeding cage and sex each batch of potential parents as they come in.'

'What about the smell?'

'The bottles don't mind.'

'Oh, you are a one. What I really want to know is how you . . . er . . . you know . . . thingy . . .'

'Sex them? I was coming to that. As you will appreciate, the difference to the naked eye is non-existent. Even with the help of a strong magnifying glass, the essential difference is not a lot to write home about. In the interests of speed, therefore – and speed is vital if we are to win another Queen's Award for Industry – we have to look for secondary sex characteristics.'

'Ooh.'

'The male bottle has a rugged, muscular exterior, shifty eyes and hairy legs, whereas the female bottle is smaller, more rounded in shape, smoother in the leg and with soft, round eyes. Once an experienced sexer such as myself has noted all these characteristics, he can be ninety-nine per cent sure. There is, of course, the occasional deviation from the norm, but this has to be accepted on the grounds of efficiency. If we worried about every female bottle with hairy legs, or every male bottle with soft round eyes, we'd never get anywhere, would we?'

'No, no. Of course not.' By this time he had forgotten all about his fodder and was practically chaffless. 'And then what do you do?'

'The female bottles I pick up gently by the offside wing with a pair of felt-lined tweezers, and place gently through the hatch into the breeding chamber. There they can wander at will over a landscape of chopped-up chicken, pulverised pig and homogenised horse, eating heartily to keep up their strength for the mating flights with the selected male bottles.

'The male bottles are treated in the same fashion, except that only exceptional specimens are allowed through into the breeding cage. And then only at a ratio of one in twenty. The rest, poor things, must await their fate.'

'What happens to the rejects, then?'

'The best of them are crated and exported by supersonic jet to countries like Greenland, where the climate is such as to inhibit the supply of wild bottles for selective breeding. We did try a sales drive in the Arab states, but they seem to have plenty of flies of their own.

'The real rejects – the undersized or not very bright, or those with blots on their escutcheons – oh, poor things...'

'Go on. What happens to them?'

'This is the part of the job I dislike most. On the sexing bench I keep a brick and a two-pound hammer. Those rejects utterly beyond hope of redemption are placed on the brick and given a swift clout with the hammer. That's when it really hurts. Sometimes the pain is unbearable.'

'You must be very sensitive. They're only bluebottles after all. They wouldn't feel a thing. So why should you feel any pain?'

'Because,' I said, 'sometimes they struggle. And I get my thumb under the hammer.'

The penny dropped.

'Hey,' he said. 'Just a minute. You're having me on, aren't you?

You're not a bluebottle sexer after all. You've been pulling my –'

'All right. All right. I confess. I can see it's no use trying to fool you.' (This time I *really* had to fix him.) 'I'm really in the pottery trade. I'm a sagger maker's bottom knocker.'

'Well, well, well,' he said. 'It's a small world. You're the second in here this week. Had one of them on Tuesday. You don't have to tell me about your job now. I know all about sagger maker's bottom knocking from what this chap told me – ooh, he did go on.'

Pause for double handful of chaff. Here it comes. Back in my ears. Up my nose.

'But – now here's an interesting thing. His brother. *His* brother.

He's a taxidermist at London Zoo. They keep him there so that when anything rare or valuable dies, they don't have to throw it away. They call him in and he stuffs it. Sometimes there and then. On the spot.

'Apparently one day an elephant dropped down dead. Heart attack. Just like that. Well, they rang this chap's brother up and they said...'

* * *

I'm still not sure whether the sagger maker's bottom knocker with the taxidermist brother did come in for a haircut. Or whether the barber was having me on. Taking the mickey. Trying to make an idiot out of me.

Some people are like that.

The curse of the cosa nostril

'See you,' said Mad Mac over the electric telephone, 'in the *Boot and Slipper.*'

'Roger,' I said. 'Over and out.'

Normally we meet in the *Queen and Cobbler*. The *Boot and Slipper* meant that something was afoot.

Mac shuffled sideways into the *Boot* with his collar up and bobbly hat pulled over his eyes, completely masking his identity. A definite improvement.

'Thanks,' he said, lifting the edge of his bobbly hat from his top lip and siphoning off a double Scotch. 'Can't stay. Walls have ears. The night has a thousand thingies. All right, then. Just one more small double. If you insist.'

I didn't recall insisting.

'There's a Contract out,' hissed Mac from the corner of his mouth which wasn't busy with the second Scotch. 'For the New Year match.'

'Gad!' I hissed. (Hissing is catching.) 'Who's going to be nobbled this time?'

'You.'

'And serve him – yer what?'

'Put me down, ol' buddy,' said Mac. 'I'm only repeating what I've heard. At great personal risk. Besides which you're spilling my Scotch.'

* * *

Contracts, as you know, are put out to nobble angling superstars. Not by the bookies, but by rival syndicates who stand to win a lot of money if the favourite loses and their own choice weighs in at first place. Any unscrupulous member of the public can take up the Contract, incapacitate the highly fancied matchman, and collect a percentage of the Syndicate's takings.

The nobblings can take many horrifying forms, from being shoved in a vat of bleach during a tour of a tripe works, to being propositioned by a young and blonde lady person in the local on a Friday night, just as the Light of Your Life walks in to collect your wage packet.

'Ta,' said Mac, putting the second Scotch out of danger. 'Slurrp. And that. Now, ol' buddy, you may think you are not worth putting a Contract out for because of the consistency of your performances in this particular annual New Year match. Like, bottom for the past five years on account of spreading the Christmas comfort and joy and overdoing the ding dong merrily. The Syndicate is cashing in on this very consistency by laying bets on your being bottom again. And the Contract is out to keep you on your usual form – i.e. lousy – for the Big Day.'

'Right,' I said. Steely and determined. 'Let them do their worst. But tell me one thing: who is behind all this?'

'Must go,' said Mac. 'I have my reputation to think of. And my remaining front teeth. Take care, ol' buddy.'

... Over the next few days I realised what it means to have a Contract out for one's own precious person. Why people in more primitive societies, such as Yorkshire, die of fright once the witch doctor has pointed the bone. Why everybody in *Treasure Island* went freaky once Blind Pew had planted the Black Spot.

You can trust nobody. Not even your best friend. Especially when your best friend is Mad Mac.

'Goodnight, Cliff,' said some shadowy figures at the bar as I left.

What did they mean, 'Goodnight'? What was that 'Cliff' bit all about? Who *were* these people?

Must get with the self defence, I decided, and next day studied a book on judo. Fat lot of good that was; the first half of the book was full of things you were not allowed to do.

You are not allowed, for instance, to pull your opponent down to start *Ne-waza*. I had no intention of starting *Ne-waza* even standing up. And you must not hold your opponent's *judogi* with your teeth. I should think not. You never know where it's been. Nor may you untie his trousers without the referee's permission. What the hell goes on at judo classes?

That evening, with the help of Number One Son, I prepared to brush up on the more traditional methods of self defence.

'Right, me old fruit. Prepare yourself. Papa is taking a refresher course in the noble art of grunt and groan. As seen on telly every Saturday. Get out of that. I learned it from the Dynamite Kid.'

Number One Son got out of it with a real nasty.

'I learned that,' he said, 'from Tally Ho Kaye.'
Ooh, me back.

* * *

... Soon it was obvious that I was not going to be nobbled by physical violence. The Syndicate's methods were much more subtle. The next day's post brought a letter from the bank manager. Report to the National Westminster in shirt-tail order for a telling off about your feckless and spendthrift habits. Wonder how much the Syndicate was paying *him*?

Then a brief note from the telephone people. Don't call us, and we can't call you because we're cutting you off.

Letter from Cousin Jim from Leeds, enclosing old family group he found among his photographs. Thought I might like it to bring back memories.

Right at the front of the group, in full, massive and indescribable horror, sat – the Mother-in-Law! Aaaaargh! Jim lad, what are you trying to do to me?

Go for relaxing drive in faithful old motor car to get away from it all. Number plate falls off in front of large policeman who slaps his hand on nearside wing, putting it straight through the fibreglass disguise job I'd done to pass the MOT. I'd have him know I have friends in high places, except he obviously has friends in higher ones.

Back in the *Boot and Slipper* that evening. Trying to forget. When silken-haired bitch name of Zena snuggles up, chews my ear and lays her head on my shoulder.

Good job Zena's only a spaniel, I'm thinking, but let that be a warning. I am heeding the warning very seriously when a real live lady person sits next to me and asks, 'How about that drink you promised me six months ago?'

This is it. The Big One. The Great Temptation. Resist it, Parker, lest hidden cameras record your every move.

'Not tonight, darlin'. I'm expecting the wife.'

'I *am* the wife.'

Eek!

Night before the Big Match. Early to bed. To sleep the sleep of the just. Drifting away. Little pink clouds. Then blissful-type unconsciousness. Until three in the morning.

EEEEEEOOOOOOWWW!!!

Wassat? Wassat? Daft cat, Jemima - who is not quite right in the head - carousing with boyfriend, Bumface, right underneath the bedroom window.

Run downstairs in State of Nature. Apart from vest. Out through the front door. Fall over milk bottles. Throw milk bottles, including note asking for One Small Double Cream, in general direction of caterwauling.

Et tu, Jemima. Which is latin for I'll break your flaming neck when you come in.

No more sleep that night. But who needs sleep? Spend time checking tackle and bait and practising Parker Patented Match-winning Lightning Strike.

* * *

Get to water a bit baggy under the eyes, a touch frayed around the edges, but in fighting mood. Big Cliff's a-comin'. Giving nasty looks to stewards and opposition, all of whom are doubtless in pay of the Syndicate. But by now they know better than to meddle with Parker. He's mean.

Clifford John . . .
Big bad Jo-hohn . . .

The day wears on. And tension mounts. Some Cleverclogs three pegs down nets four pounds of fish. Which anybody can do at *that* peg. But at the Parker peg it takes skill to - STRIKE!!!

Gottim gottim gottim! Two ounces if he's a dram. You lovely little perch, you. Give us a kiss . . .

Anyway, I'd done it. Not exactly top - second from bottom if you must know - but bottom no longer. I'd beaten the Syndicate. It could stick its Contract up its Cosa Nostril.

* * *

'. . . Bygones be bygones,' I said to Mac later. 'Even though you did desert me in my hour of doodah. Have a pint.'

'On me,' said Mac. 'Out of my winnings.'

'What winnings? You didn't back that rank outsider with the four pounds of pure fluke?'

'No, ol' buddy. I backed you. Side bets, five to one, that you wouldn't come bottom this year.'

'But ... the Contract?'

'Forgive me. A small fabrication. A little less than the absolute truth. In the cause of applied psychology and some side bets at five to one. I thought that if I got you rattled enough you might actually pay attention and catch something. You had me worried, though ...'

Mac is now as well as can be expected.

... being extracts from the diaries and other documents of the Sludgethorpe Waltonians. This from the diary of Chukkitan Chansit, the club's Pakistani member.

See Blackpool and live

We are having a most jolly weekend by the sea: all the Waltonians together on a club outing.

It is the idea of my good friend Harry Turner, who was asking last week that the social funds be used for this purpose before the Committee are getting their sticky fingers on it. Although the implications of Harry's words are not well received by the Committee, the suggestion is being proposed and carried.

The advance party is leaving Sludgethorpe on Friday night for Blackpool, a town I am very much looking forward to seeing, since Harry said that if I had not been to Blackpool I had not lived.

I am most impressed on arrival by all the happy people walking up and down wearing hats with naughty suggestions printed on the front, and by the big Tower, which is looking very much like the one in Paris only with the legs cut off.

We are dropping the luggage at the Happidays Holiday Flatlets and following Harry to a working men's club, which he is entering by waving his Sludgethorpe membership card and shouting 'Affiliated!' to the gentleman at the door.

Such a very elegant working men's club I am never seeing before: the members must be working very hard to afford the organ and the automatic bingo ball dispenser.

We are sitting at several tables, all the advance party from Sludgethorpe, and soon a very smart waiting man is bringing us lots of bhoose and we are having jolly laughings. Then there is a roll of drums and some noise from the organ. A gentleman in a glittery suit, whom Harry is identifying for me as the Emsee, is asking for order round the room and a big hand for our very own Booboo Nookie.

Booboo Nookie is a blonde and plump young lady in a most immodest garment, who is bouncing up and down and singing lots of songs very loudly but not very much in tune. I am not enjoying the singing very much, but Harry is saying that with a dress like that, who is caring about the singing?

Miss Nookie is eventually going off, after a deep and most shocking bow, to the accompaniment of much clapping and whistling.

'How do you think we shall be doing at the fishing tomorrow?' I am shouting to Harry above the noise.

'You never can tell, Chuck,' he is saying, staring very intently at Miss Nookie. 'But I've got my name down for a couple of whoppers . . .'

I am waking up on the Saturday morning in the Happidays Holiday Flatlets with a most penetrating pain in my head and a very strange taste in my mouth. It is some comfort to discover that Harry is suffering likewise. This most uncomfortable condition is apparently normal in circumstances of severe hanging over.

Harry is asking me to be having a hair of the dog that bit me and to be taking a swig of the Scotch before we are setting off for Fleetwood, the Las Vegas of the North. I am saying no thank you very much to the hair of the dog, but by the time we are on the tramcar to Fleetwood, I am thinking that anything is better than the rattling of dry brains, and am most gratefully taking the swig.

At Fleetwood, which is not looking very much like Las Vegas, we are meeting the overnight party from Sludgethorpe, which is including our distinguished chairman, Mr Harbottle, and such others as were unable to join the advance party.

On the beach we are meeting our boat, which is not the biggest I am ever seeing, and which is grounding itself front first on the sand. I am wondering how we are to be climbing aboard, when a ladder is dropped over the side by a very pleasant gentleman who is our Mr Skipper. This ladder is not looking very Bristolshape and shipfashion, being only the front end of a pair of stepladders.

Harry is saying, 'Get up first, Chuck, and grab the seats at the back.' I am attempting to do this when our distinguished chairman pushes in front of me and mounts the ladder. Silly old bhooger,

Harry is saying, when the ladder is slipping and Mr Harbottle is making distressful noises.

I am jumping into the water and holding the ladder steady. This move is allowing Mr Harbottle and several members of the Committee to climb into the boat and take possession of the seats at the back. Also it is allowing my boots to fill with water and my trousers to be getting wet up to the knees, and beyond into places where the cold water is most unwelcome.

Harry is grabbing me and pushing me up the ladder, himself following close behind and making uncomplimentary remarks about the behaviour of the chairman and Committee.

'Never mind, Chuck,' he is saying as we settle ourselves in the middle of the boat. 'If they're up to their usual form, they'll be catching nowt anyway.'

After sailing for some time we are anchoring and getting the rods over the side. The genial Mr Skipper is coming round for some happy chats and is telling us that we are likely to be catching the plaice, dabs and whiting, and to be careful of the whitings' teeth, which are apparently most dangerous.

Mr Harbottle is being the first to make a catch with a little dab. Harry is saying doesn't it make you spit, when I am hearing a shout from Clogger Sedgewick, who is fishing with Tupper Brown from the other side of the boat.

'Whiting! Whiting!' Clogger is shouting. I am saying please to be watching the teeth. Clogger is saying what the bloody hell do I know about it, when he is suddenly giving a cry of great pain. As Mr Skipper is putting a bandage on his finger, which has been severely bitten by the whiting, Clogger is shouting to me that I suppose I think I am very clever and just wait till his hand gets better.

On Harry's advice I am making no reply to this, but am concentrating on the fishing. Suddenly there is a snatching at my line and the rod is bending very strongly downwards. Tupper Brown is giving an excited shout because he too is having the bite, but I cannot concern myself with his situation.

Harry is telling me to be pumping the fish and giving it some stick, and I am doing both most manfully. There is a cry from Mr Skipper to be hanging on a bit, but Harry is saying to be giving it the hammer and one last big heave will do it.

I am giving it the hammer with one last big heave when there is a loud noise from Tupper Brown and a large splashing on the other side of the boat.

'Man overboard!' my fellow members are shouting, and Harry is laughing most heartily.

'You've got a good one there,' he is saying. 'Fourteen stone of wind and water - you've just pulled Tupper over the side!'

I am realising that my line must have drifted under the boat and become entangled with that of Tupper's. I am now most concerned for his safety.

'Don't worry, Chuck lad,' Harry is saying. 'I'll throw him a line.'

He is picking up a rope which has a bucket tied onto the end and throwing the rope to the unfortunate Tupper. Tupper is being more unfortunate when the bucket is hitting him on the head.

'It's all right,' Harry is saying. 'He's only been down twice. He's got one more go before his wife can collect the divi.'

As usual, Harry is correct. Tupper is coming up for the third time, grasping the rope and being hauled aboard. He is not seeming at all grateful and is trying to kick me in a most sensitive spot. Harry, in my defence, is hitting him with the bucket. This time the bucket is full of water and is being most effective in knocking Tupper unconscious.

Harry is trying to look concerned and is calling for volunteers for the Kissing of Life. Meeting with no response, he is making the compromise by filling the bucket again with seawater and throwing it over Tupper. This is doing the trick and waking him up.

Mr Skipper is saying that he is not minding the joke but to be sodding the pantomime, and he is thinking we should get back before anything drastic is happening.

Now Harry is attracting my attention, most surreptitiously. 'When we land at Fleetwood,' he is hissing into my ear, 'let that lot get on the first tram back to Blackpool. You and me will catch the second tram and stop off for a few pints of Pemberton's Old and Filthy.'

... So we are catching the second tram and are now in a very jolly hostelry with a concert room and posters advertising all-star lunchtime cabarets. After two pints of Pemberton's Old and Filthy, a thought is striking me.

'Harry,' I am saying, 'when you were telling me to give the fish the hammer and one last big heave, were you knowing that my line was tangled with that of Tupper?'

'No Chuck,' said Harry. 'Nay, lad. Would I ever do a thing like that? Still, I'm glad we're back early. I wanted to see a man about a dog.'

I am looking around the room to see if there is a man with a dog, when suddenly there is a noise of organ and drums, and an Emsee is leaping onto the stage.

'Cabaret time again at the *Pig in a Poke*, folks,' he is saying. 'And I want you all to give a big hand to your own – your very own – Miss Booboo Nookie!'

Suddenly everything is coming clear to me, and I about to give Harry some pieces of my mind.

'Sssshhh . . .' he is saying, staring most intently at Miss Booboo, who is bounding onto the stage and singing most loudly. 'And not a word to Vera . . .'

Hokamapokus and the Indian death lock

Hot, it was, unusual for an English Summer, and all the fish seemed to have shifted to one part of the canal. Big pike, bream, perch, roach, a couple of small carp and hundreds of gudgeon and minnows were just lying there, none of them stirring.

I had tried everything - every bait known to man and the last ounce of my angling skill and daring - and had not a touch all day.

Pondering this later in the *Boot and Slipper*, I concluded that skill, expertise, knowledge, intelligence, long years of experience and breathtakingly good looks were not enough. What this problem needed was some supernatural help. Some magic. Some of the old ackamarackus and hokamapokus.

Mad Mac, I thought. He's the lad.

Mac, you see, is very good on spells. Not all of them work: our mothers-in-law are still around to prove it. But some of them do. He once put a curse on his bank manager and the bank manager caught a very bad cold. It was three years later but, as Mac pointed out, it only went to prove the strength and staying power of a curse well cussed.

Right, I thought. I will this very minute get on the electric telephone and ask him round. No sooner had I thought it than there was Mac standing in front of me, as if he had shot up through a trapdoor like a little Demon King.

'Mac!' I cried. 'This must be extra-sensory perception! What metaphysical powers have brought you here in my very hour of need?'

'Shucks, 'tis nothing, ol' buddy,' said Mac. 'I tuned in on your astral wavelength and divined that you have a spare tenner which I need urgently if I am to stave off total penury, a raging thirst and possibly sudden death.'

Gad, what powers the lad has. There was indeed a spare tenner. Not exactly spare - I had gently eased it out of the housekeeping money on a short term loan - but there it was.

'It is a privilege to lend it to you,' said I, handing it over.

'Isn't it?' said Mac. 'Now, ol' buddy, is there any small service I can render you in return?'

I explained about the state of the canal and Mac applied his gigantic intellect to the problem, making no sound except to cough gently when his pint pot was empty. When it was full again, he spoke.

'What you have been doing, ol' buddy, if you will forgive my frankness, is using obvious methods and obvious baits to pursue an obvious quarry which obviously could not have cared less.

'Those fish are lying there, uncaring and unheeding, because they are, in marine biological terms, knackered. The combination of water temperature and de-oxygenation has reduced their metabolic functions to a point where food has lost all its interest. The fact also that they can see the loony, if you will pardon the expression, who is chucking grub at them, is another counter-productive factor. What we have to do is . . .'

Mac's voice tailed off, and he stared thoughtfully into the bottom of his empty mug. When I'd refilled it, he started again, gathering speed like an old wind-up gramophone.

'. . . go after them in places where they least expect it, using baits of an irresistible and exotic nature, enlisting also the aid of my own million-dollar brain.'

Whoever put up the money for Mac's brain was conned. However, he outlined a plan which seemed eminently sensible and worth the price of a few more pints.

Firstly, when I got home that night, I was to perform my justly famous Hopi Indian rain dance, which had never been known to fail except in times of drought. This I did, on the back lawn, and was rewarded by a flash of lightning which would have been the first of many if Dearly Beloved had not dragged me back indoors in case the neighbours complained.

Secondly, I was to prepare the Parker Secret Superbait, a deadly and inimitable mixture of catfood, sugar, chip butties and finer flour with graded grains. To which, on the morrow, Mac was to add a few drops of Doctor Dumdum's Electric Wonder Oil, a compound of seal oil and sulphuric acid which he had bought in bulk from a little Indian with a turban in a pub near Hemel Hempstead. Doctor Dumdum's not only cured every illness known to man and had saved the Eskimos from extinction, but it was also irresistible to fish.

* * *

On the morrow, we arrived at the canal. Mac announced that he was going to use his powers as a dowser to pendulise the water. His pendulum was a human tooth tied on the end of a piece of cotton. Well, not quite a human tooth. It was one of Mac's.

What we were to do, said Mac, was to stop every twenty-five yards along the towpath to dangle the pendulum. If the tooth went round and round, it meant that there were no fish present. If it went backwards and forwards, it meant that the fish were there in their thousands.

Mac demonstrated first at the spot I had tried the day before, and which was still packed with comatose fish. Sure enough, the pendulum swung backwards and forwards.

'All we have to do now,' he said, 'is to move along the canal until it wags at a spot where we *can't* see the fish. Where they're feeding in secret.'

Marvelling at the lad's powers, I followed him along the towpath. Every twenty-five yards or so he stopped and pendulised. Every time, the tooth went round and round, indicating a chronic lack of fish. We must have gone threequarters of a mile, by which time I was buckling at the knees on account of carrying the tackle for the pair of us, when Mac exclaimed, 'This is it, ol' buddy!'

His pendulum was swinging back and forth at a rate which indicated that the water must be jammed solid with fish, yet not a one could we see.

All a-tremble, I set up my rod - and Mac's as well, as he was still busy pendulising - and used the Parker Secret Superbait, enhanced with Doctor Dumdum's, on the hooks.

At the end of an hour, there had been not a nibble. I turned round. 'Mac -'

Mac was nowhere to be seen. Probably, I thought, pendulising the full length of the Grand Union to make sure of success. What a mate. What a lovely ol' buddy. What a - Hang on. Wait a minute . . .

For the first time I noticed that I was fishing near the lock gates which led across to the *Hole In The Bucket*, a pub which featured ale of outstanding qualities and barmaids of the same. The stretch of water leading up to the lock was known to the locals as Boot

Hill, on account of anything living in that stretch being dead. If you follow me.

Something was amiss.

Hoppity-skip, I went, across the lock and into the pub. Where against the bar leaned Mac, gazing at the barmaid's outstanding qualities.

'Another large Scotch, please, darlin',' he was saying. 'And one for yourself. Ah – here comes my ol' buddy, fresh from his massive and miraculous draught of fishes. What are you having, buddy mate?' Then his voice dropped to a whisper. 'And could you lend me some of the folding stuff on account of I am temporarily financially embarrassed?'

Control yourself, Parker.

'Apart from the massive and miraculous draught of fishes,' I said, 'for which later I am going to tear you limb from limb, you had a tenner from me last night. Which I could ill afford on account of having filched it from the housekeeping.'

'Believe me, ol' buddy, I do understand,' said Mac, oozing sympathy and sincerity. 'When I got home, my ever loving wife had four quid of it away on account of I had done the very same thing.'

'What about the other six quid, then?'

'Ah. Well. Let me see. How can I put it? Not to beat about the bush. To coin a phrase. And come straight to the point. I've supped it.'

* * *

... Mac complained that the Indian Death Lock I applied to his neck made him walk with his head on one side for three days afterwards. But I reckon he got off lightly. The Indian Death Lock which Dearly Beloved applied to my neck when I tried to explain about the tenner made me walk with my head on one side for a full week.

I did learn one thing, though: the art of pendulising. To make the pendulum go round and round, you twist the cotton between your thumb and middle finger. To make it go backwards and forwards, you give it a surreptitious flick.

Then you look for a mate daft enough to believe in it.

In my own rite

I like my tea hot, strong and in a pint mug. It's an indication of character, is that. Shows I'm dead common.

I realised just how common when I saw this lad on the telly, dressed in full Japanese gear, demonstrating the Japanese Tea Ceremony. There's more to it than sticking the little finger in the air and not cooling the tea in the saucer. The whole thing is a ritual, right from the brewing of the tea, the kind of pot and cup you use, to the way you pour it and drink it.

The aim of the ritual, which is about 900 years old, is to bring on a contemplative mood, and to bring hosts and guests into perfect harmony. There are even different forms of ceremony for different times of the day.

Even more interesting though was the fact that the lad on the box - who was about as Japanese as I am - makes a living from demonstrating and lecturing on the ceremony.

Suddenly a whole new career opened up in front of me: demonstrating to a waiting world the ancient British angling ceremonies. It wouldn't cost me a penny in costumes: I'd already got 'em. Apart from a couple of items I could rescue before the dustbin men came round.

Already I could hear the television chat show host:

'Our special guest tonight is the distinguished British angler, Mr Cliff Parker, who will demonstrate the age-old rituals associated with his mysterious art.

'Mr Parker is wearing the traditional angler's costume: Man United bobbly hat; anorak decorated with abstract designs formed by the action of gravity on draught bitter and cheese sandwiches; baggy and low-slung trousers and broad-soled wellies with a hole in each toe.

'We shall be talking to Mr Parker later, but first let us look at the ceremonies recorded by our outside broadcast cameras on a typical day's fishing.

'The ceremonies start early in the morning. This is the *Public Transport Ceremony*. You can see the bus pull up, and Mr Parker place his basket, holdall and nets on the platform. Now you see the conductor ceremonially throw them off. With a few time-honoured old English words, Mr Parker replaces them on the platform and steps on after them.

'The conductor now performs a tricky triple movement: he shoves Mr Parker off the platform, kicks the gear into the road, and rings the bell. As the bus moves off, Mr Parker picks himself up, stretches to his full height, and raises his right hand with two fingers widely spread in the traditional Angler's Farewell.

'The approach to the water is crowded with ritual. Here we see Mr Parker performing the *Stile Leaping Ceremony*. There he is at the top of the stile, executing a graceful high kick with his right leg. Listen now to the strange cry he emits between clenched teeth and notice how his eyes suddenly fill with tears.

'See the climax of the ceremony as his left foot slips and he clears the stile in a graceful parabola, falling in a carefully controlled heap.

'Watch him as he crosses the field, performing the *Cowpat Skipping Dance,* very much akin to the Scottish sword dance; slipping now and again as he makes the inevitable miscalculation. See him speed up in the *Bull Running Sprint* as the lone bullock in the field turns out to be in full possession of its faculties.

'At the water he performs the dangerous *Bank Walking Ritual,* carefully avoiding all the hidden holes. Apart from the last one, which leads him naturally into *Welly Emptying and Trouser Wringing*.

'The next few ceremonies are self explanatory: *Tree Tangling* (note the accuracy with which he casts his bait into the topmost branches); *Pike Disgorging* (note the sudden absence of fingers on the right hand); and *Packing Up* (note the power of his movements as he kicks his basket up and down the bank).

'We follow him into an ancient British hostelry for the *Fibbing Ceremony*. See how wide he spreads his arms to an enthralled audience. And in that one, remember, he is only demonstrating the size of the bait.

'This is followed, as always, by the *Drowning of the Sorrows.* Note the time-honoured Dead Man's Grip on the pint pot. Mark the movement of his Adam's apple in the highly disciplined Triple Slurp. See how the froth sticks to his nose and a dribble of amber

liquid runs down his chin to add to the intricate patterns on his anorak.

'In *Well Past Time* he is joined by the landlord of the hostelry, who escorts him to the door and pushes him symbolically into the street with the ritual chant, "And don't come back!"

'Now we see him outside Parker Manor, his stately home, for the ceremony entitled *You Find Out Who Your Friends Are.* Obviously in some form of ecstatic trance, he is supported by his stalwart comrades, Mad Mac and Big McGinty. They prop him carefully against the front door, ring the bell and run away.

'Finally, what must be the most touching ceremony of all: *Return of the Wanderer.* The door is thrown open by an unseen hand. Keeping absolutely rigid, Mr Parker falls inside, flat on his face.

'Now we see *Mrs* Parker, in all her fiery beauty and curlers, welcoming him with the words; "And where do you think *you've* been till now?' Mr Parker opens his eyes and with a beatific smile murmurs, "Hello, Petal," before relapsing into his trance.

'Mrs Parker grasps him by the collar and, with practised ease, drags him up the hallway. His wellies disappear over the step, and the door closes behind them.

'Further ceremonies were enacted inside, but these were of a strictly private nature. And, as you can see now in the studio, from Mr Parker's split lip and pronounced limp, very painful . . .'

An angler's farewell to his welly

Hail to thee, blithe welly!
Boot thou never wert.
But part of me angling person,
At the other end from me shirt.

Brings tears to me eyes, that does. It's the first verse of *Ode to a Welly,* which I wrote after laying my faithful old pair to rest.

The welly doctor looked at them and said, 'Well, the left one's all right, but there's nothing I can do for the other one. That hole in the toe is too far gone. And there are signs of perishment around the welt.'

'You mean – ?' I choked.

'Afraid so. There's nothing for it but to have her put down.'

I still wouldn't give up. 'You're not giving me a load of old doctors are you, cobbler?' I hissed, grabbing him by the awls.

'No, son,' he said. 'She's paddled her last, has that one. It would be a kindness.'

Now one welly is no use without the other. I have enough trouble as it is without having to hop everywhere. So I decided that they would go together. As doubtless they would have wished.

Getting rid of a pair of wellies poses a problem. The dustbin would be too humiliating, too undignified, after all their years of loyal service. I thought of burying them in the garden, beside the compost heap from which they had helped me dig thousands of the world-renowned Parker Pike-Strangling lobs. And perhaps put a little headstone on top with a suitable inscription:

Farewell, farewell, old wellies.
I couldn't part from thee.
Until one of you got a hole in the toe
And squelched cowflop up to me knee.

On second thoughts, no. Non-welly persons would not understand. Perhaps even think I was not the full shilling.

Burial at sea would have been romantic, but I couldn't afford the

Awayday ticket. Apart from which, the Grand Union Canal would have been more appropriate. However, the thought of their being hooked up at some time by a total stranger, to the accompaniment of ribald laughter from his mates, was too horrible to contemplate.

In the end I gave them a Viking funeral. Chucked them in the garden incinerator. It was a very spectacular and fitting end, even though the smell and clouds of black smoke brought threats of lawsuits from the neighbours. And a few stern words from Dearly Beloved, who had just pegged the washing out.

Served me right, she said, that for a week my underpants would smell like barbecued knicker elastic.

* * *

To ease the pain, I've since been working on *Ode to a Welly*. Don't see why not, if Keats could write one to a soppy nightingale he'd never even met.

How's this, recalling the time I sat on the bank, contemplating my toecap?

How goes it with thee, old welly?
By gum, we've seen some life.
Tha's protected me through thick and thin,
'Cept once, when swung by the wife.

It wasn't the welly's fault, though. The swinging was done after I'd splodged through the house, leaving a trail of mud on the carpets that Dearly Beloved had just vacuumed. Women get touchy sometimes about the strangest things.

Then there was the time when my faithful wellies pounded o'er the greensward (as they say in the better class of poems) to put some distance between me and a large grass-eating animal with pointy things on its head:

Hey up, watch out, old wellies!
Just look what that silly cow's done.
By 'eck, it's a bull, old wellies!
Dost tha fancy a bit of a run?

Remorse always sets in at a time like this, and I can't keep back the memory of what was probably the beginning of the hole in the toe:

My fault, I suppose, old welly.
Tha may have lived a lot longer.
If, way out at sea,
I hadn't let thee
Get bit by a bloody great conger.

Finally, as a last salute to the stricken right welly, a nostalgic recollection of one Enchanted Evening:

Remember the time, old welly,
We went night fishing with that stripper?
She filled you with rum,
Fell flat on her bum,
And left me supping gin from her slipper.

It's not true, that. Tell the wife. I just made it up. And perhaps that's why I'll never make the charts as a poet. I always finish up lowering the tone.

Fish safe with Piffle

Nothing like an enjoyable day's fishing, is there? Fresh air, healthy exercise, the pursuit of a cunning prey, the companionship of fellow anglers at the end of the day. Ah, me.

Shame that it can be spoiled by little things, silly mistakes that even the most skilful angler can make in moments of forgetfulness or inattention.

The Parker Institute for Failsafe Fishing and Long-term Enjoyment (PIFFLE) has researched out some of the commoner happenings and their causes. Take this check list with you next time you go out as an instant guide to where you are going wrong:

HAPPENING. On climbing over a stile, you give a high kick at the top. Suddenly you are lying in a recumbent and undignified posture, possibly also in something nasty, with all your gear piled on top of you.
CAUSE. You didn't kick high enough. Watch how Rudolf Nureyev does it on the telly.

HAPPENING. On climbing over a stile, you give a high kick at the top. This results in excruciating pain, watering eyes and a funny walk.
CAUSE. You kicked too high. Who do you think you are – Rudolf Nureyev?

HAPPENING. After walking past a grazing cow, you become aware of a steady drumming noise, a tremor in the ground, and a feeling of flying.
CAUSE. The cow was a bull. At your age you should know the difference. Or at least change your glasses.

HAPPENING. You sit down on your basket, fall over backwards, and find your wellies clamped around your ears.
CAUSE. You left the basket lid open. Get out of that.

HAPPENING. You sit down on your basket and rise immediately.

About six feet in the air. Screaming blue murder.
CAUSE. You sat down on your rod rest. The basket's over there.

HAPPENING. You launch into a championship-length cast, but fail to see the splash as the terminal rig lands.
CAUSE. Championship-length casts are seldom necessary on the canal. Search the field across the bridge. Alternatively, look in the trees behind you.

HAPPENING. A pleasure boat swishes past at well over the speed limit, cutting your line and causing a wash which knocks hell out of your keep net. You throw a bottle at the skipper, and immediately burst into tears.
CAUSE. The bottle was full.

HAPPENING. You are into a whopper, get it close to the bank, draw it over the landing net and *hup*! – where the hell's it gone?
CAUSE. You didn't screw the net onto the handle before you started. Statistics show that a handle without a net is significantly less effective.

HAPPENING. You pull in the keep net to take out a cool can of beer, and find the net empty.
CAUSE. You never did get around to mending that hole in the bottom.

HAPPENING. During a quiet spell, you fill your pipe from the tin beside you and light it. There are several loud explosions and a smell like barbecued horse manure.
CAUSE. Mistaking the feel of the sawdust for your favourite brand of ready-rubbed, you filled your pipe from the bait tin. The soft bits were maggots. Console yourself with the thought that they felt no pain, but *look* next time. And for God's sake stop that coughing.

HAPPENING. After giving one with the rod rest to the dog scoffing your groundbait, you are aware of a splintering sensation on your bobbly hat and flashing lights before the eyes.
CAUSE. In your anger at the dog, you failed to notice the large lady

with the brolly who was walking the thing.

HAPPENING. After giving up in disgust, you pack your gear and stomp off up the towpath. Suddenly you find yourself soaking wet, covered in green slime, and staring into the eyes of a very puzzled duck.
CAUSE. You had memorised the location of every hole and crumbling bit of bank along the towpath. Except that one.

HAPPENING. Later that night, after a few pints to restore your shattered nerves and hurt feelings, you notice that the wall of the bar is decorated with nicotine-stained lampshades and that it is moving slowly past you.
CAUSE. Having overdone the sedatives, you have fallen flat on your back and are being transported to the door by some of the landlord's trusties. The nicotine-stained lampshades are those on the ceiling.

HAPPENING. You get home in a foul mood, fall over the milk bottles, drop-kick the cat and play hell with the wife.
CAUSE. Almost certainly the stress of the enjoyable day's fishing. Never mind. You'll know better next time...

... being extracts from the diaries and other documents of the Sludgethorpe Waltonians. This from the battered typewriter of Ken Scratcher, ace (and only) reporter of the *Sludgethorpe Echo.*

The camera can't lie

I've achieved the ambition of every reporter – to write a novel and get it published.

I'm glad I was sensible and stopped trying to write another *War and Peace,* and turned instead to the people and situations I know about.

I based the book on the Sludgethorpe Waltonians. Not that anything exciting ever happens to them, apart from the occasional absconding treasurer and some post-match punch-ups, but you have to start somewhere.

I like the publisher's blurb:

THE THIRTEENTH PEG

A saga of sex and violence beside the still waters!
The loves and hates of a band of dedicated anglers!
The passions and conflicts beneath the placid surface of an everyday angling club!
WHO poisoned the beer on social night?
WHAT was going on in the shrubbery behind the clubhouse?
WHO killed the ace matchman the night before the all-important contest?
WILL any of them survive the Big Match Massacre?

The publishers had an idea for the cover. Stark, sordid, brutal realism, with just a touch of fantasy.

'We'll shoot the club,' said the art director.

'Isn't that going a bit far?' I asked.

Jokes like that are wasted on some people.

He would send a photographer all the way from London, said the art director, to shoot the members on location, all lined up outside the clubhouse. That would be the stark, sordid, brutal realism. The touch of fantasy would be four nubile lady persons, wearing less than a little, mingling with the members.

'Do these girls know what they're in for?' I asked. 'I wouldn't trust our cat with some of that lot.'

'Don't worry,' he said. 'They're professionals.'

There was no answer to that.

Down came the photographer with the four beauties. Complications set in straightaway. When the girls removed their coats, there was a distinct possibility of the steamier bits of the book coming true. Mr Harbottle, the chairman, had to be treated for palpitations and one of the junior anglers fainted on the spot.

Lulu Waghorn, young and lovely wife of the former chairman of the Veterans' Committee, had heard about the girls and turned up in a microscopic bikini. This brought the colour back to the cheeks of ace matchman Chalky White, but it didn't do much for the photographer.

'Would the lady with the dyed hair and spare tyre mind putting some clothes on?' he drawled. Lulu rushed off in tears and locked herself in the Ladies with a bottle of gin.

The scantily dressed girls took up their positions in the ranks. One was told to caress Harry Turner's cheek and look smoulderingly into his eyes. She must have over-smouldered, because she let out a loud shriek and gave Harry a fourpenny one. Another girl was having trouble with old Harbottle, which came as a surprise to everybody. Especially old Harbottle.

The photographer took three or four shots, then he said, 'Now, sweeties, let's get with the realism. Let's make with the brutality. You two, ruffle your hair and scowl. You - yes, you, the old gentleman who's making a nuisance of himself - take out your teeth and leer. Chappie over there - let's have that sheath knife where we can see it. The butch chappie next to him - one with the tattoos - hold that rod rest thing like a dagger...'

So it went on. The sight at the end would have turned back a herd of stampeding rhino. I've seen some rough spectacles in my time, but this really put me off my grub.

The photographer packed up, prised the girls loose, and waved an elegant farewell. Lulu was lured from the Ladies with a promise of appearing on next year's club calendar. And everybody was happy. For a week.

Then I had a phone call from old Harbottle.

'I have in front of me a letter from a photographic agency in London,' he said. 'They happened to see the results of our little session and would like to use the club members as regular models in future. It's disgraceful! It's humiliating!'

'What do you mean?' I asked. 'Surely it's a compliment?'

'Not,' said Harbottle, his voice quivering with suppressed rage, 'not when the name of the agency is *Mugs and Monsters*!'

There's no pleasing some people.

Ollie and Stan meet the werewolf

'I've got this tent,' said Mad Mac. 'Picked it up dirt cheap at a sale of cheap dirt. Now we can go night fishing.'

Oh no. Anything but night fishing with Mac, the walking, talking, all-singing, all-dancing Disaster Spectacular.

It's not just that things happen to *him*. Perfectly innocent and inoffensive people all around are being run over, mugged, dropped in twelve feet of water, thumped in pubs or having things dropped on them from great heights. And all they did was get too close to Mac.

A couple of years ago he walked into the bank to cash a cheque. He wondered why the manager was standing there with his hands in the air, and was upset by the lack of response to his demands for service. He was threatening to take his overdraft elsewhere when he noticed the four big lads with stockings over their heads, waggling guns and swinging pick handles.

'Ah,' said Mac, polite as always. 'I take it you were first.'

Then he met a sad little feller in a pub. The bloke's wife had either just left him or just come back to him, he'd lost his job and the bailiffs were due any second. There was nothing to laff at at all.

'Cheer up,' said Mac. 'Have a pint and start thinking positively. Look at the beautiful blue sky out there. See that sun streaming through the window? And listen to those tweetie birds. Isn't it a wonderful world?'

The little bloke agreed, cheered up, finished his pint and left the pub whistling a happy tune. Three seconds later he was back, hopping up and down and clutching a shattered right boot. A lorry had run over his foot.

At one time I myself had accepted the fact that life was real, life was tough, life was cruel. Life was full of hazard and strewn with pitfalls for the unwary. All that changed after I met Mac. Life became much simpler. Sort of . . . what's the word?

Horrific.

So I said no way will I go night fishing with you, ol' buddy. Over my dead body. Wild horses will not drag me, nor all the riches of the Orient tempt me. Go away. Get lost. Visit your friendly neighbourhood taxidermist.

* * *

We got to the water late on Friday night.

'Tackle up first,' I said. Me being the angling brains of the outfit. 'We don't want to miss any of these monster pike.'

'Are you sure we're in the right place?' asked Mac. 'It's pitch dark.'

'I can see that,' I said. 'But I wasn't a platoon scout for nothing. In one of the Service Corps' crack units.'

'I know that, ol' buddy,' said Mac. 'And no disrespect. But the bit of the Empire you were defending was one of the first to go.'

'Shurrup,' I said. (I'm a bit touchy about that. Wasn't my fault, entirely.) 'Where's the torch?'

'I thought you had it.'

'Can't I leave *anything* to you?'

I struck a match and flicked it away from the bank. Its reflection glistened below. Then it disappeared with a sudden hiss.

'See,' I said. 'That's the water. Now where's the bait?'

Mac took the tie off a plastic bag that opened with a pong like a long-lost Billingsgate sewer.

'Here we are, ol' buddy.'

'Phew! Hak hak! I thought you said you'd got *fresh* herrings.'

'They were fresh when I bought 'em.'

'And when was that?'

'Last Tuesday. Or was it Monday? No, I tell a lie . . .'

'Oh, give 'em here!'

Tackle up, bait up and cast out. Rod rests and buzzers fixed up. All done by touch. Smashing. Now for the tent.

'You'll pardon me,' said Mac. 'But I'm in charge of pitching the tent. It being mine, and that. We'll have it just here.'

He unrolled the tent and spread it out. 'Be careful,' he said, 'that you don't step on the fabric. It'll let water in.'

'No need to tell me that,' I said. Stepping off it.

All it cost to put up the tent was a busted hammer shaft (Mac's), a flat thumb and a split finger (mine). Success. In we crawled.

'I thought you said this was a two-man tent,' I complained. Not that I'm one to complain.

'That's right, ol' buddy. Says so on the label.'

'Where did you get it – Mothercare?'

'You'll get used to it. Have a Scotch.'

Now and again Mac says something sensible.

The tent started to warm up. Before long there was a fug. A fug to end all fugs. I struck a match, which illuminated Mac's lucky socks.

'I am not having those feet in here with me,' I said.

'I can't leave 'em outside, ol' buddy. They're attached to me legs.'

'Couldn't you stick 'em through the flap or something?'

'It is a well known scientific fact,' said Mac, 'that smelly feet are a sign of virility. Irresistible to women. If that scent gets out onto the night air, we'll be attacked by hordes of little darlings. After our bodies. Crazed with lust.'

'When was the last time you were attacked by hordes of little darlings, after your body and crazed with lust?'

'Pass the wellies,' said Mac.

* * *

Time passed. Not a buzz. Another Scotch? Ta. Hark!

'Wassat? Wassat? Outside the tent! Breathing heavily!'

(I am normally very cool in moments of extreme peril, but reserve the right to panic now and again.)

'Nothing, ol' buddy,' said Mac. 'Just some old cow.'

'Perhaps you were right about those feet.'

'Or mayhap the Mad Hatchetman of Leighton Buzzard,' he mused. 'Prowling the countryside in search of fresh victims to quench his insatiable thirst for blood.'

'Eek!'

'Or a wandering werewolf. Who has stopped taking the tablets and is doomed forever to follow the trail of –'

'Shurrup. Since you're so brave, go out and see what it is.'

Mac was just starting his excuses, based on an allergy to werewolves and a lack of empathy with mad hatchetmen, when a great twanging of guy ropes and a pained 'Moo!' identified the monster beyond all reasonable doubt.

'Shoo, shoo!' we both cried. 'Away with you! Sod off!'

I failed in my attempt to chuck Mac through the flap as the Ultimate Deterrent, mainly because he'd got a leg scissors on the tent pole.

As it turned out, his sacrifice would not have been called for.

With a final twang and a scrape, the poor old cow was off, galloping up the field, probably to scare her mates out of their tiny minds with stories of werewolves and mad hatchetmen.

'See?' said Mac. 'Nothing to be afraid of.'

* * *

More time passed. Still no buzz. Another Scotch? Ta.

'Silly question, ol' buddy,' said Mac. 'But how many of us are there in here?'

'Two. At the last count.'

'I think we've got company. Something just moved under this groundsheet. There it is again!'

'There's bound to be a simple explanation. Keep still and listen.'

'What for?'

Eek, eek.

Rats.

'Aaaargh!' yelled Mac. 'Can't stand em! Wanna die! Lemme out!'

'Har har. Serves you right. Bloody werewolves. And who was it masterminded the pitching of this tent? Right over the little ratties' front door?'

Mac's screaming and thrashing about sent the rat back down its hole like a shot. He was in no danger, after all. He could always have stuffed his lucky socks under the groundsheet and gassed it.

A couple more Scotches and he felt better. Still no buzz from the rods. Outside, a lone tweetie bird made with a few lonely tweets. A faint glimmer of light. The first rosy fingers of dawn. Get outside, Parker, and see what's happening to the lines.

. . . Oo-er. Dear me. Well, I'll be. That is to say. Bloody 'ell.

'Don't bother coming out, Mac. It's cold out here. I'll just reel in and see how the baits look.'

The baits looked great. Which was understandable because they'd been lying all night, untouched, in a couple of inches of water on the edge of a cow drink on the far bank. Any pike which reached them would have to have been a pole vaulter.

Reel in both baits and cast out again into a respectable spot. Before any aspersions can be cast on my night-fishing skill.

Mac's head sticking out of the tent.

'Anything doing, ol' buddy?'

'Of course not. What did you expect with those geriatric herrings?'

'Sorry about that.'

'I should flaming well think so.'

'I won't do it again.'

'You'd better not. Wasting a whole night like this. Me having to put up with werewolves, hatchetmen, old cows, flaming rats and your hundred-year-old feet. And what for? Nowt. All my pike-fishing skill and experience to no avail. The last chance of the Season, too. All because you didn't have the sense to get the bait yesterday afternoon instead of . . .'

Mac scratched his head, his eyes filled up, and his mouth turned down at the corners.

'I'm sorry, Ollie.'

'I should think so too, Stanley. That's *another* fine mess you've got me into. Hm-*hmm*!'

. . . It's a great double act, that last bit. One of these days it might catch on.

The secret of Idiots' Reach

There is a stretch of the River Lune, near Lancaster, that I'm very fond of. Beautiful, it is, with a slow, curving run and densely wooded banks.

I only wish there were some fish in it.

I tell a lie. There are salmon and sea trout, whoppers, leaping about tantalisingly in the middle. And, on other stretches, shoals of gigantic bream. But on this stretch by the bank . . . nowt. It's known to the locals as Idiots' Reach.

'I can't understand it,' said Cousin Jim from Leeds. 'Five years I've been fishing this bit, and never done owt to speak of.'

Between us, Jim and I have tried everything but hand grenades. And if Jim can't catch anything, it *is* bad. He has a caravan near the river, is down there most weekends, and is a master of the Noble Art to boot.

I've seen Jim in action on the Swale, where he can not only get a barbel at first trot, but tell you in advance how big it is, what its name is, and whether it sleeps with its whiskers inside or outside the covers.

Obviously, if Jim's getting nothing from Idiots' Reach, there must be a Secret.

I thought I had it once when a local, further down the bank, said, '*Worms*, lad. Big 'uns. That's the secret.'

Now *he* was having some modest success. Not a lot. But pulling in the odd undersized bleak or roach.

I wondered how he managed that with giant worms. At the end of the week I found out: he was using maggots. The advice about worms was strictly for the suckers.

Cousin Jim was on the verge of solving the mystery when he met an elderly local in the pub.

'I'll tell thee t'secret, lad,' said the Ancient. 'Only one way to do it. The secret is . . . The secret is – Aaargh!'

And the poor old feller flaked out with a heart attack. It must have been a goodie, because he's not been back since.

* * *

Up at Idiots' Reach again for a week's fishing, I was determined to crack the secret. Straight round to the tackle shop for river licence, day tickets and a king's ransom of maggots and groundbait.

I'd forgotten since the last visit. The first words on the day tickets are: NO GROUNDBAIT ALLOWED. Not that it stopped the enterprising tackle dealer selling it. And further down, in the small print: 'No fishing before eight a.m. or after eight p.m.'

With no groundbait, and no fishing at the best times of day, it's a bit restricting. The bloke in the tackle shop must be making a fortune out of groundbait that's never used. But is it never used?

Round about seven o'clock one morning, I noticed a bloke throwing balls in the river for his dog to retrieve. The dog swam out all right, but never came back with any of the balls. Funny.

Then there were several blokes taking early morning swims. Was it imagination, or did they come out thinner than they went in? Was there something stuffed down the front of their cossies? Such as a plastic bag full of bran and breadcrumbs?

There seemed to be a lot of feeding the ducks going on, too. The ducks had to work very hard, trying to catch up with the bread. It went straight down to the bottom, almost as if it had been soaked and squeezed.

And all those anglers walking the bank just before eight a.m., loaded with tackle. Trying to look as if they were just going fishing when, from the look of the damp keep nets, they'd just been.

'I suspect a spot of the old foul play,' I said to Number One Son. 'But I daren't indulge in it myself. I've got my reputation to think of.'

'What reputation's that then, Dad?' he said.

Ho ho. *Very* droll.

* * *

On the last day, just as I was packing up, an old boy with thick specs came tottering down the bank.

'Evening, young sir,' he said. (You can tell why he wore the thick specs.) 'May I ask how you're doing?'

It was a good job he was a bit deaf as well. He missed the first string of expletives and caught the more polite account of the week's activities.

'There are plenty of good fish left in this river,' he said.

'I know,' I said. 'And I'm the bloke who left 'em there.'

'There's a secret,' he said.

'Quick,' I said, remembering the old lad who flaked out on Cousin Jim. 'Sit yourself down on my basket. Have a fag. Swig of Scotch?'

'Thank you kindly, young sir. Most civil of you. Yes, what was I saying?'

'The secret. THE SECRET!!!' I yelled. As calmly as I could. Fighting down the impulse to shake hands with his neck.

'Ah, yes. It's so simple, really. Lots of groundbait. And fish first thing in the morning and last thing at night. I've had no end of stuff like that.'

'But the rules.'

'What rules?'

'On the tickets. No groundbaiting. No fishing before eight a.m. or after eight p.m.'

'Really? Must be something new. Mind you, my eyes haven't been very good for thirty years. I can't read anything smaller than a hoarding. But never mind what it says on the tickets. I've told you the secret. Think on.'

He got up from the basket and tottered up the bank, raising his cap to a gatepost as he went. Leaving behind him The Secret. And me. Sobbing.

I wouldn't say I was bitter about it. But where I spat, nothing will ever grow again.

Stand by for blasting

I can see it now. My epitaph:

HERE LIES PARKER,
KEEN AS MUSTARD,
CUT DOWN IN HIS PRIME
BY EXPLODING CUSTARD.

Don't laugh. This is serious. (On second thoughts, do laugh. It might be the only chance you get.)

There was a horrifying safety report on a custard explosion in a British food factory. Injured nine blokes, it did, and well-nigh wrecked the place.

And here's me, all these years, happily slapping custard powder in the groundbait as one of the secret and deadly ingredients. (Perhaps it doesn't do much for the fish, but *I* like the smell. So there.)

What happened at the factory was that a fault in the custard powder machine caused cornflour dust to collect in the air. The same fault caused a spark and – *Boom!* Nine blokes flat on their backs. Let's just hope they were believed when they phoned their Ever Lovings:

'I'll be a bit late home tonight, love. The custard's just exploded.'

'A likely story. You'll have to do better than that if you don't want your tea on the fire-back.'

It was a freak accident, of course. Otherwise we'd never sleep for fear of being sent to the Great Beyond by an exploding vanilla slice. But to be on the safe side I've resolved to use less volatile additives.

You try it – try and find a powdered ingredient which won't explode, given half a chance and a naked light – and see what you come up with.

Production at a continental factory went with a bang when sugar dust in the air exploded. 'Quite a number of organic dusts, and even metal dusts, will, if mixed with air in the right quantities, burn with excessive violence,' said the safety report.

Among the dusts listed, along with cornflour, were cereals such

Graham Allen

as barley, wheat or rice, coffee, cocoa and bran. How many of those have you mixed together in the same groundbait? The coroner would have a hell of a job to determine which one caused your premature demise. And when he'd finally made up his mind, what a verdict: *Death by misadventure and combustible cocoa.*

Sawdust, too, is potentially explosive. So be careful how you take the lid off your tin of maggots. 'I should do well today, Sid. I've got some right little beaut –' BERDOOM!!

And what about the scene at the Pearly Gates after an international match? Poor old Saint Peter would hardly have time to check all the lads in before the Last Trump:

'Get fell in! Three orderly ranks! Cocoas on the right, Sawdusts in the middle and Brans on the left. Come on, move yourselves! I haven't got all Hereafter!

'That man there! Why aren't you in line? You're what? Pigeon Droppings? You trying to be funny, laddie? No? All right, then – get over there with the Cocoas. I'll never get through all this paperwork if I have to fill in a separate form for every semolina, marzipan and pigeon dropping freak.

'And look at me when I'm talking to you! If you must stand there with your head tucked underneath your arm, at least get it tucked the right way round.'

Pigeon droppings? Yes, they're explosive, too. Chicken droppings certainly are, so there's no reason why pigeon droppings shouldn't be. It's a wonder there aren't dozens of tourists in Trafalgar Square exploding from direct hits every day.

Even desiccated coconut isn't to be trusted. Not since the news that the Philippine army has successfully exploded a coconut bomb.

Still, there are always the non-powdery groundbait additives to fall back on: honey, syrup, treacle. But what have we here in the Stop Press? News of exploding treacle tins. If they're left in store, chemical changes in the treacle give off gas which can blow the lids and send the tins flying from the shelves.

That's all you'd need. After successfully avoiding being struck down by custard, sugar, cocoa, rice, bran, sawdust and pigeon wotsit, to be clobbered by a flying tin of treacle.

What's known in the trade as a sticky end.

The Blackpool rocky horror show

Came back from holiday hoping to report record-breaking catches and lots of jolly fun and adventure.

But no. Only doom, disaster, failure, tragedy, horror, and a vague feeling that perhaps things didn't go quite as well as they might.

I had gone up to Blackpool *en famille,* apart from Daft Cat, for a week's spiritual regeneration. You know the kind of thing: cartwheels across the sands at seven in the morning, singing the old Al Jolson numbers to the seagulls, lunchtime ale at *Uncle Tom's Cabin* and the prospect of pulling out some big fish, hopefully non-radioactive, from Morecambe Bay.

But every silver lining has a cloud. And the biggest cloud was waiting for us at the digs – the Mother-in-Law.

Shock! Horror! Wanna be sick!

Booked in for a week, she was. A fifty-million-to-one chance. Purely by a fantastic coincidence. And the fact that she'd found out where we were staying.

I'm not saying anything against her, mind. A lovely woman. Even though she was thrown out of the Gestapo for brutality. (Only kiddin', Ida. Gerroff me neck.) She was a model, you know, in her younger days. For Toby jugs and door knockers. Some people say she's sharp-featured, but that's only because she's got a face like a bag of chisels. And big! She's the only woman I know with wall-to-wall feet. Whenever she goes down on the sands, the tide remembers a previous engagement. If she walks down the street, all the weighing machines jump back inside the chemists. Last time she stood on a speak-your-weight machine it said, 'One at a time, *please*!'

At the very least, though, her appearance was an omen of disasters to come. And they were not very long in coming.

It started with Number One Son. Or at least his queasy tum, which will not allow him to step across a puddle without seasickness setting in.

Number One Son is a lovely lad. Tall, dark, handsome, muscular and highly intelligent. Which he gets from his dad. But he cannot sail or fly without the collywobbles setting in. Which he gets from somebody else. Possibly his mum, who has been known to turn a funny colour on a park boating lake.

'Right, me old fruit,' I said, outlining the plans for the next day. 'On the morrow, at crack of doodah, we embark at Fleetwood, taking the morning tide to high adventure. Coming back with enough protein-packed fish to feed us and Daft Cat for a twelvemonth.'

'Papa,' he said. (Having had a good upbringing and knowing how to address th'owd feller.) 'Papa, I simply couldn't. You know how bad I was on that trip out from Brixham.'

'This isn't Brixham,' I replied. 'This is Morecambe Bay. Calm as a millpond. Flat as my wallet. The sea doesn't go up and down like it did at Brixham.'

'Excuse me,' he said. 'I think I'm going to be sick.'

So that was that. No boat fishing. We tried North Pier at Blackpool and he stuck it manfully, although he did feel poorly just looking through the cracks in the planks. After three days, nothing had happened. Not a bite. The mockers were well and truly on . . .

There was still hope. Cousin Jim from Leeds was staying with his lovely Philomena and the kids in their caravan on the banks of the Lune.

'Bags of fish,' he said over the electric telephone. 'Come up for a day and try it.'

Into the car. Me, Dearly Beloved, Number One Son and Darling Daughter. Apologies to mother-in-law about lack of space for her – but promise to send a skip if she really wants to come – and off to the Crook o' Lune. Get plenty of fish there, all right, while the womenfolk twitter about in the caravan.

Greetings over. Cousin Jim and his young Richard, me and Number One Son, all ready with the tackle to go down to the river.

'Just a minute,' said Jim. 'That horse tied up over there has got the rope wound round its back leg. I'll go and untie it.'

The horse, a big one, was staked out at the top of the field, which was a big one, too, and which sloped steeply towards the river. Cousin Jim, though in good fettle, is not exactly built like Mister Universe. I had the feeling that the omen was still omening, that mother-in-law still had her mojo working.

Jim pulled the stake out of the ground and unwound the rope from the horse's leg.

'Nowt to worry about,' he said. 'All you've got to do with these things is be firm. Show 'em who's boss.'

Just then, a mare whinnied down by the river. The horse gave a fruity 'Wahahaaay!', reared up on its hind legs, and shot off down the field at full gallop.

Jim showed who was boss by hanging onto the rope and shooting six feet in the air. He looked like the first bionic man on the Moon, bounding down the field on the end of the rope and touching the ground about every five yards.

He was giving out with expert noises of command like, 'Whoa! Give over! Pull up, yer bugger!' Every time one of his feet touched the ground, these commands were interrupted by, 'Ooh! Ouch! Eek! Aaaargh!'

The horse reached the mare on the river bank and stopped dead. Jim kept going and cannoned off the cush. He turned a double somersault – worthy of a Ten for Perfection – and finished flat on his back.

His eyes were tightly closed when the rest of us reached him. And he was still clutching the rope, being dragged from tussock to tussock as the horse pranced around.

I prised the rope from his lifeless hand and tied it to a bush.

'Speak to me, dad,' pleaded Jim's young Richard. 'I've not had me spends yet.'

Jim's eyes opened.

'All you've got to do,' he croaked, 'is show 'em who's boss.'

We helped him to his feet and dusted him down.

'Never mind, Jim lad,' I said. 'You did a grand job. Now just come down the bank and we'll get with the fish.'

'Right,' said Jim. And put his best foot forward.

'Eeeeaaaarrrrgh!'

'Wassamatter? Wassamatter?'

'I've done meself a mischief!'

'Not in front of the children, James.'

'Every time I move my legs I get dreadful pain right up to my–Eeeeaaaarrrrgh!'

Jim was obviously not well. Number One Son and myself picked him up by the elbows and carried him up the field and into the caravan, where the lovely Philomena was distressed to hear of the injuries, and even more distressed to hear of their location.

We loaded him into the car and unloaded him at the local doc's, chanting 'Accident! Emergency! Life and death!' to get priority over the summer 'flu and dozyitis cases in the waiting room.

The doctor pronounced a pulling of several of Jim's muscles: the *sartorius*, the *pectineus*, the *adductor longus* and possibly even the *quadriceps femoris*. He advised rest and recuperation: no more cycling, horse riding or trampolining for a bit.

'What I want to know,' said Jim, 'is whether I shall ever play the violin again.'

'I see no reason why your prospects should be impaired,' said the doc. 'Oh - no fishing for a bit, either. A cast from a standing position could be very painful. And we don't want to do ourselves any more nasties, do we?'

* * *

'Has it ever occurred to you,' said Jim later, trying to sup a pint from a prone position in the pub, 'that for most of the year I live a quiet, uneventful life. But whenever you turn up, something dreadful happens. You were with me on the Swale when that cow fell on me. You were with me when it whoopsied all down my shirt as I tried to push it back up the bank. You were with me when I got chucked out of the pub afterwards for stinking the place out. And now this. Have you got a jinx or something?'

'I'm afraid so, Jim,' I said. 'It's in the family. On the wife's side.'

Pick a peck of pickled pockets

In an earlier chapter I discussed the angler's Outfit and its disgusting state.

One aspect of the Outfit I merely touched on: the contents of the pockets. In the earlier chapter, as here, I was talking to the ladies. To the gallant lasses who have to endure a close relationship with a coarse fisherman. Who complain for nine months of the year that they never see the lad. And then moan continually for three months because he's always under their feet.

The end of the Close Season is the time many new brides go through the pockets of their loved one's Outfit. They do it because they want their feller to go out into the new Season feeling clean, tidy, and free from last Season's encumbrances. And because they are bloody nosy.

Those of you women who have already frisked the Outfit will still be in a state of shock. Those of you who are about to frisk it ought to know what lies in store. Those of you with any sense will leave it alone altogether, but I fear there is little chance of that.

Those pockets contain the last secrets kept from woman by man. So don't say nobody warned you. What follows is a brief description of the things you are likely to find, an account of how they got there, and advice on what to do with them when you find them.

The empties. These come in two basic categories: those which held the soft stuff (light ale, brown ale, barley wine, lager, cider) and those which held the hard stuff (whisky, rum, gin, vodka, methylated spirits).

The empties which held the soft stuff are worth money at the off licence. So recover the money, put it towards a couple of full bottles of the hard stuff, and replace the full bottles lovingly in the pocket. If you can't afford the real thing, buy a couple of bottles of paint stripper: first thing in the morning he'll never notice the difference.

Mouldy loaves and petrified butties. No good to him now, and the fish wouldn't fancy them. Use the loaves as doorstops or save them for next time he has a craving for bread pudden. Use the butties to replace the roof tiles he was supposed to have fixed during the Close Season.

String of mummified sausages. A relic of his last trip out after barbel, when the barbel had gone dead off sausages. It could be that the mummifying has preserved them, and all you have to do is steam them out a bit to restore the flexibility and fry them up for his breakfast. Worth a try. Should they have gone off to the point of administering a fatal dose of swine fever, well you weren't to know, were you?

Hot water bottle. By now, possibly cold. He'll have to fill it himself before he goes out, so just empty it and pin it to his lapel where he can find it.

Cigarette packets. Usually holding one or two broken fags or a collection of tab ends. Put them back. Otherwise, three months since he last wore the jacket, he'll be reaching into his pocket and saying, 'Funny. I could have sworn I had some fags in here the other day.'

Floats, shot containers, hook packets, disgorgers, maggot tins and dead duck. Leave everything where it is except the duck. He'll need all the gear, but he won't have much use for the duck, which may well have gone off a bit. And he'd only be filled with remorse, (a) at the memory of pinging it one with his catapult when it went for his groundbait, and (b) because he'd forgotten to give it to you when he came home. Don't let anything upset him at this highly sensitive and emotional time of the year.

Lucky socks. You've been warned about these before. Don't touch. Leave them to fester. They'd only fall to pieces if you did take them out. Then you'd be in *real* trouble.

Lucky charms. Socks apart, these could be anything from a Cornish piskey or a rabbit's foot to a pig's ear or a shrunken head. Put them all back carefully, especially the shrunken head. This may have some sentimental value, such as it once belonging to the match steward who disqualified him for breathing in last Season's semi-finals.

Cakes of soap. These could be a tribute to his fastidious personal habits, or an invaluable aid to his match technique.

False beard and ginger wig. He uses these to fish incognito, either because he is so famous it gets embarrassing, or because he's barred from so many waters. Possibly for using with the cakes of soap as an aid to his match technique.

Marked cards and loaded dice. It wouldn't do any harm to make sure that the cards are in good condition – i.e. haven't been nibbled by mice, affected by mould, aren't crumpled or faded. Dust any affected cards lightly with french chalk and put them back in the pack.

Check the dice: even when thrown on a forty-five degree surface, they should drop with a definite plonk and show a six apiece.

He may need both the cards and the dice to recover his match fee and ale money on the Season's first trip out with the club. He's only thinking of you: it saves it coming out of the housekeeping.

Satin bra and frilly knickers. These are possibly not yours. If the labels read *Fanny's Soho Knickerama,* instead of *St Michael* or *Taylor Woodrow,* it gives you a clue. And possibly you've never worn a bra with tassels. Nor bikini briefs, preferring to stick to the tried and trusted passion killers on account of the draughts around your neighbourhood.

Do not jump to conclusions about your find. These are what he uses as aids to fine fishing. The bra makes a comfortable double-chamber micromesh keep net for gudgeon of restricted growth. And the pants might have been designed for the specific purpose of straining bloodworms, so well do they perform that age-old and honourable function.

Apart from that, he may have found them on the bank and kept them in case the owner turned up to claim them. Apart from that, they may be his lucky charms.

And he's going to need all the luck he can get if he can't think up any excuses better than those.

A pat on the back

There's a fascinating study course run at the Preston Montford Field Study Centre near Shrewsbury.

The Ecology of a Cowpat, it's called. And as a lady person who was making a six-month study of the subject so aptly remarked, 'It's really quite interesting when you get into it.'

As one who has been into as many cowpats as the average angler, I can vouch for that, and I would like to make my contribution to the March of Science by offering a few observations on *The Cowpat, Its Dangers and Its Uses*. Not only may these observations be of use to the layman, they may also save a beginner or townie angler from unnecessary embarrassment or discomfort.

To begin at the beginning. Cowpats are made by cows, bulls and bullocks. As it is difficult to differentiate between a cowpat, a bullpat or a bullockpat, all three are referred to simply as cowpats.

Generally a tasteful brown or green colour, cowpats go through three stages:

1. The Squishy. This is a new cowpat, and at this stage is at its most dangerous. An angler stepping in one tends to do a back somersault and land in the same spot. Hence the phrase: A pat on the back.

2. The Crusty. At this stage, appearances are deceptive. What looks like a firm crust is merely a thin layer concealing a Squishy interior. Though the crust cuts down the incidence of back somersaults, you can't always depend on it.

3. The Set Hard. These offer no danger, and are the ones to be prised up when you're in search of wild bait. All sorts of maggots, grubs and creepies live under there, and they can come in very useful if your own bait runs low or the fish are being fussy.

As well as having amazing powers of lubrication underfoot, both the Squishy and the Crusty have amazing powers of adhesion. However much you wipe your feet, there's still some left on when you get to the pub. This leads to dirty looks from other customers and requests from the landlord for you to stand out in the yard.

There is usually still some pat remaining by the time you get home, which can result in your wellies being thrown halfway down the garden by your Ever Loving. Sometimes with your own dear self still inside them.

But a pat on the foot, and even a pat on the back, pales into insignificance compared with a pat in the face. Rule One for anglers fishing a country venue is: Never go to sleep in a field.

Cows are either absent-minded or anti-social, or both. More than one angler who has settled down for forty winks on a hot summer afternoon has been absent-mindedly anti-socialled on. The result might look like a mudpack but it doesn't do the complexion an awful lot of good.

Anglers into camouflage can use the cowpat as a substitute for mud to darken the face and reduce the flash from a bald head. Such anglers tend to finish up writing to the agony columns about their lack of friends and wondering why their wives don't understand them.

With the Set Hard pat we have something completely different. If the fish aren't biting, the pats can be used as frisbees to while away the time. Some anglers have even tried to play them on portable gramophones, but they tend to work only with the old 78 needles. A diamond needle, or even a sapphire, is inclined to shred them and muffle the tone.

Anyone purloining cowpats for home consumption – for use on the compost heap or in the wormarium – is advised to take only the Set Hard ones. They're much lighter, easier to carry, and stack better in the boot of the car. And if the farmer approaches, you can stick one on your head and pretend it's your cap.

Here, begging to be let in, is the joke about the angler who lost his cap in a field of cows. He tried on fifty before he found it.

(What do you mean – 'And then what happened?' That's the joke. Think about it.)

The use of a cowpat, even a Set Hard, as a cap substitute on any long-term basis is not to be recommended. They're fine in the hot, dry weather, but at the first onset of rain they turn soggy and droop over your ears, leaving you looking like Deputy Dawg and ponging like Pepe le Pew.

One final use of the Set Hard is as fuel for a smudge fire to keep the midges away on the bank. It certainly works. Kills midges by the thousand. Tell you what, though: it doesn't half bring the tears to your eyes.

A bit like this piece, really . . .

. . . being extracts from the diaries and other documents of the Sludgethorpe Waltonians. This from the diary of Horace Harris, the little quiet feller.

The Sludgethorpe swan upping

I had to agree with my good friend Harry Turner that the swans on Jackson's Clay Pit were getting a little obstreperous. As Harry was in bed at the time, nursing the results of a vicious and unprovoked attack by Charlie, the oldest and largest of the swans, I could hardly do otherwise.

Old Charlie had been on the pit for as long as I could remember, and had always made a nuisance of himself, stealing groundbait and butties and hissing at or pecking anybody who dared to remonstrate. The other swans had picked up his anti-social habits, and the poor Sludgethorpe anglers had to brave mass attacks every time they fished the pit.

Now then, I tell a lie. Charlie normally hissed at or pecked everybody but Harry. For some reason, perhaps not entirely unconnected with Harry's skill with a half-brick or landing net handle, he kept well clear. Until that fateful morning when Harry had to answer a Call of Nature.

Charlie must have sensed that he had Harry at a disadvantage. He cruised silently along to the spot on the bank where Harry was answering the Call, and struck. He pecked Harry hard on a sensitive part of his person, sending him leaping in agony up the bank, and necessitating the application of witch hazel, and a cold compress to get the swelling down.*

'That,' said Harry, from his bed of pain, 'is that. There's only one thing to be done with the swans on the pit. Up 'em.'

---

*It is surprising how sensitive and how susceptible to swelling one's kneecaps can be.

'Come, come,' I remonstrated gently, looking around in case Harry's Vera was in earshot.

'No,' said Harry. 'I'm being serious. You've heard of the Thames Swan Upping every year, where the swans are caught for marking to make sure everybody knows which belongs to who? Or whom? That's what we'll do at the pit. Up 'em. But instead of marking them, have them carted off to a good home somewhere else. I know the very bloke.

'Now, not a word to anybody about this. There may be the odd bit in the small print of the pit lease which would stop us carrying out an official Upping. You and I, with the help of my swan fancier contact, will up 'em unofficially. For the sake of the club, old friend.'

As he mentioned the club, tears sprang suddenly to Harry's eyes. I thought that was ever so touching and agreed without hesitation. The magic of that moment will stay with me for ever, even though I discovered later that the tears were the result of a misplaced hot water bottle.

* * *

I had to meet Harry outside the pit at the crack of dawn on the following Monday morning. Harry had chosen Monday for reasons of privacy. Nobody fished the pit on Mondays because (a) it was a working day, and (b) it was hangover day for most of the Waltonians. Though our expedition would make us late for our highly skilled jobs at Sludgethorpe Plastics, Harry had arranged for Chukkitan Chansit, our little Paki mate, to clock in for us.

At the pit we were greeted by a quick flash of headlights from a plain van which was parked, unlit, under some trees. A little man emerged, carrying what looked like a shepherd's crook.

'I'd like you to meet Mr Doggett, of the Vintners' Company,' said Harry. 'An expert on Swan Upping.'

'By Appointment,' said the little man. 'My card.'

It was too dark to read, so I slipped the card into my pocket.

'Put these on,' said the little man, and handed Harry and myself a nylon stocking each. He had one himself, and pulled it over his head.

'Camouflage,' he said. 'Essential that the swans do not see the whites of our eyes.'

He also produced a dozen sacks, each with one of the bottom corners cut off.

'What we do,' he said, 'is to hook each swan with this crook – we get 'em by hook or by crook, if you get my meaning, har har – and bung it into a sack so that its head sticks out of the hole in the bottom. That stops its wings flapping about. All you've got to do then is to watch out for its beak.'

Harry winced. Obviously the memory lingered on.

... It only took an hour to get all the swans bagged and in the back of the van. I must admit that I wasn't much help, not being able to see clearly through the stocking over my head, but Mr Doggett had obviously done this kind of thing before. The Vintners' Company, I seemed to recall, was one of those which provided the Swanmasters for the annual Thames Swan Upping. 'By Appointment', too. We were obviously in the hands of an expert.

'What a nice man,' I said to Harry as the van drove off with the cargo of swans. 'I'm sure those birds will enjoy their new home.'

'They'll never know what hit 'em,' said Harry.

It was now light enough to read Mr. Doggett's card. It read:

Sid Doggett,
Manager,
Vintner's High Class Poulterers and Tripe Dressers,
Knacker's Yard Close,
Sludgethorpe.
(By Appointment Purveyors of Tripe and Cowheel to Sludgethorpe Trades and Labour Club.)

Not quite the Vintners' Company I was thinking of, but obviously a reputable establishment.

* * *

'You got a bird ordered for Christmas?' asked Harry, as we approached Sludgethorpe Plastics.

'Not yet,' I replied.

'Well don't bother. I'll get you a good 'un.'

'Turkey?'

'Not exactly. More like goose. And it won't cost you a bean.'

'How do you manage that?'

'Ask no questions, get told no lies,' said Harry. 'Let's just say it fell off the back of a van.'

There's a pal for you.

* * *

I must say the fishing at Jackson's Clay Pit has improved no end since the swans went. There was a bit of a hue and cry when their disappearance was first noticed. Ken Scratcher, the *Sludgethorpe Echo* ace (and only) reporter, wrote a front page story on the mystery, concluding that the long dry summer followed by a monsoon-like autumn might have influenced the swans' life patterns, or upset their biological rhythms, and caused them to migrate to more settled climes.

PC Arthur Mow investigated and questioned several members of the Waltonians, including Harry. But as he questions Harry as a matter of course every time so much as a tomcat goes missing, nobody thought anything of it.

I am looking forward to Christmas now that I can enjoy a decent-sized bird. I had resigned myself to a chicken from the supermarket.

And I do hope that the swans have settled down in their new home. Wherever it is.

Psi in the sky

'I can't understand it,' I said to Mad Mac as we prepared to leave the water. 'That's the second week running I've packed up my gear to find that the rod rest's bent.'

'Perhaps you need a lighter rod,' said Mac.

'Hardly,' I said. 'The damn thing's bent upwards.'

'Parapsychology,' said Mac.

'Pardon?'

'There's been a lot of it about lately, ol' buddy. *Psi,* we call it in the trade. The unknown. The unexplainable. And that.'

'Such as?'

'Telepathy, for a start. You've probably noticed how we both decide to pack up fishing at the same time. Telepathy, that is.'

'It's not. It's because the pubs are open.'

'Which just goes to prove,' said Mac. 'We both know the pubs are open, even though neither of our watches work. And why? Because we're picking up vibrations from the landlord.'

'Give over. He doesn't even know we're here.'

'Exactly. But he's putting out unconscious messages into the ether to get some customers in. He doesn't want to be standing there like a spare part, lonely as a cloud, with all that ale lying unsupped in the cellar.'

'But which landlord? There are six pubs within lurching distance of here.'

'The landlord who's giving off the strongest vibrations. Six pubs, OK? But we'll only be going into one of them. How do you think we choose?'

'If you discount the one that doesn't allow anglers, the other one with the mucky pipes, and the third one we're barred from on account of the spectacle you made of yourself the other week, it's usually the nearest.'

'Oh, ye of little faith,' said Mac, waxing biblical. 'Let's try another example. OBE.'

'That's a medal.'

'Wrong. It's an Out of the Body Experience. You know, when you leave your body and can watch yourself doing things.'

'That's roughly why we got barred from that pub. Except that in your case it was more an Out-of-the-Mind Experience.'

'Be serious,' said Mac, wishing to stay off the subject of why we got barred from that pub. 'Take ESP – Extra Sensory Perception to you. It's very common, for instance, to know your float is going to bob a split second before it actually does. And to know, for another instance, that it's a perch that's taken it.'

'Got you there,' I said. 'I've been into that one. When your float bobs, you go into a brief state of shock. Often you can't remember striking. When your mind puts the bits back together again, it seems as if you knew it was happening before it did, but you didn't. And you know it's a perch because you can feel it jagging, only you didn't know before you felt it, although you thought you did. To put it another way –'

'Never mind,' said Mac. 'You've got your knickers in enough of a twist as it is. Psychokinesis.'

'And the same to you.'

'Psychokinesis,' steamrollered Mac, 'is the power to move things or change things without physical effort, simply by using the untapped resources of the mind.'

'I suppose that was your excuse when you knocked your pint over in that pub. Just before we were asked kindly to vacate the premises.'

'No, it's absolutely genuine. Remember Uri Geller, that lad who used to bend spoons? That's how he did it. And I reckon that could be happening to your rod rest.'

'I don't think Uri Geller fishes this stretch.'

''Course not, you fool,' said Mac. '*You're* doing the bending.'

'Give over.'

'True as I'm standing here,' said Mac, sitting down. 'Just think of all the concentration you're putting in while you fish. All those powerful beams of psychic energy concentrated on your float. What is more likely than that your rod rest, which is made of ferrous metal – iron to you – is acting as a natural conductor, channelling all that cosmic force and having its crystalline structure changed as a result?'

'Hey, I'd never thought of that. I'll straighten it out and try again.'

'Now?' asked Mac, paling.

'Why not?'

'The pubs are open.'

'For once I can miss a couple of pints in the interests of science and human advancement. Where would we be today if Edison or Marconi had nipped out for a quick one in the middle of their experiments? Or if Beethoven had just gone *Da-da-da-DAH*... and chucked it?'

'How long will you be?' asked Mac, twitching a little.

'As long as it takes. You can go on without me.'

'But I'm skint. Not a sou.'

'Hard lines. So am I. You can get some ale on the slate.'

'No I can't,' said Mac, twitching a lot. 'Not after the unfortunate incident of the psychokinetic cheque. I'll need you with me.'

'Look,' I said. 'You started this. Now I'm going to finish it.'

'OK,' said Mac. 'I give in. I cannot tell a lie. It was I who bent your rod rest.'

'You what?' I expostulated (a thing I do not normally do in polite company). 'You bent it? Two weeks running?'

'Yes,' said Mac. 'Opening those big party cans of ale. I lost the can opener and didn't like to tell you because it was yours in the first place. So I waited until you'd gone for a Nelson Riddle and opened the cans with your rod rest. Tough metal on those big cans...'

'You 'orrible little man! Why didn't you use your own flaming rest?'

'Well, it's a new one, isn't it? Aluminium. And it's got those special extending wotsits on it. Cost a lot of money, that did. I didn't want to bend it opening some crummy – Hey! Steady on, ol' buddy! I'm your mate – remember?'

... Mate or no mate, there are more ways than one of bending an iron rest.

Must tell old Uri. Save him a lot of brain fag.

You'll be a man, my son

I read a survey in *Woman* magazine about what women think makes a real man. And anglers come out of it pretty well.

Not that I read *Woman* magazine regularly, of course: just happened to pick it up in the dentist's, that's all. Says he, flexing his biceps, spitting in the fire and kicking the cat.

Not that anglers figure much in the survey, either. In fact they're not even mentioned. But judging by the answers to the questions, they're the kind of men the women would fancy if only they knew it.

Jewellery, for instance. Women don't go for too much jewellery on a man. They don't mind their blokes wearing a wedding ring or signet ring, but they do draw the line at earrings.

Anglers seldom go in for jewellery. Even wedding rings may be taken off by dedicated night fishers: just in case they get snagged in the tackle, you understand. And usually the only angler seen wearing an earring is the one sitting in the casualty ward waiting to have the spinner taken out of his shell-like.

The spinner was put there in the first place by a cack-handed cast from his mate. That's his mate sitting next to him, waiting to have the rod rest unwrapped from round his neck.

Make-up on men is another thing women don't go for. Only seven per cent would tolerate mascara, and only three per cent would put up with lipstick.

An angler's Ever Loving doesn't have much of that to worry about. She may get a shock sometimes, though, if he's been using dyed maggots and transferred some of the dye to his finely-chiselled features. Not that it's a deliberate attempt at ornamentation. All it shows is that he's given to ear-scratching and nose-picking.

Smell is another thing women are pretty positive about. Nine out of ten don't mind a smell on a man if it's called 'aftershave'. But change it to 'perfume' and two out of three don't like it.

It's a pity the survey didn't mention things such as draught bitter, cheese butties, sweaty socks and bream slime, but doubtless they were taken for granted as real masculine smells, guaranteed to turn any woman weak at the knees.

The women interviewed weren't all that keen on blokes messing about with their hair. Dyed hair, very long hair or wigs were definitely out. Doesn't affect us, anyway, because anglers have only two basic hairstyles. There's the Drowned Yeti look - basically shaggy but plastered down with slime or mud and decorated with the odd bit of duckweed - and the mature man's Egghead look, sometimes deliberately plastered with mud to eliminate flash on sunny days.

Handbags for men are out, but twenty-two per cent of women would allow their blokes to carry shoulder bags. Few anglers carry handbags, or live long enough to carry them twice, but many of them go in for the shoulder-strapped tackle basket. This, however, is OK gear: nobody can look sissy with one shoulder six inches lower than the other.

Only one in ten women minded their blokes crying privately, but a third of them would object if they cried in public. This is one area in which the average angler falls down, given as he is to the occasional display of emotion, though most of his public sobbing fits are brought on by rage or frustration.

The three main causes are: (a) drawing the peg on Gudgeon's Graveyard; (b) lifting up the keep net to discover that the beer cans have slid through the hole in the bottom; (c) arriving at the pub after a three-mile hike to discover that Time has just been called.

Now, the real nitty gritty: what attracts a woman to a man? Here, anglers really score.

Sense of humour was top of the poll with thirty-seven per cent. Anglers are noted for their superbly developed sense of humour. ('Har har - Sid's just fallen off the bridge and drowned himself . . .')

Kindness came a close second. Though their treatment of their nearest and dearest may leave something to be desired, anglers are certainly very kind to their mates. ('Look - if I bought you a pint now, you'd only want another in a few minutes, and you're skint. So I'm doing you a kindness by telling you to bugger off . . .')

Dominance polled only one per cent. Which is just as well, because for all the angler's macho image, he's not very good at it:

'Where's me tea, woman? Is it cooked yet?'

'It ought to be. It's been on the back of the fire for two hours.'

There were some strange answers, though. Such as:

'I like a thoughtful man. He must be trim shaped, especially his bottom.'

What thoughtfulness has to do with the shape of your bum, I'm still trying to work out. But then came the real killer:

'I can't stand men who smoke, have a beer gut and swear.'

Nobody's perfect, I always say...

Keep going, you fool . . .

It was no surprise to learn from a scientific paper that fish on the whole are pretty dozy, preferring to take life easy and seldom getting excited. But it *was* a surprise to learn that salmon and trout are as dozy as the rest.

The Atlantic salmon, for instance, prefers to move at speeds of less than one body-length per second. He speeds up during the spawning run, of course: can't wait to get with the action. (Younger anglers will know the feeling. Older ones will at least remember it.) But for the rest of the time the salmon is quite content just to potter around.

Experiments on brown trout by an Aberdeen University zoologist showed that a trout's heartbeat is usually slow and regular. It approaches the maximum rate only one per cent of the time. Obviously it doesn't get many electricity bills, tax demands or threatening letters from the bank.

Just one square metre of river bottom holds enough food to keep a trout for a week, so the fish spends more than half of its time stationary, with its ticker ticking over gently.

It does get upset, however, if it is caught and returned to a strange part of the water. Anxiety sets in and its heart goes like a trip hammer until it finds its way back home. The heart of one trout in the experiment went pitter-pat for two and a half days: not only did it have a dicky heart, it also had a lousy sense of direction.

Now and again the trout's heart will actually miss a beat. This happens when a shadow crosses the water or when a fly is cast above it.

The number of missed heartbeats will be going up if the methods advocated by an American angler are more widely adopted. In his book *Fishing Dry Flies for Trout on Rivers and Streams* (that's not the whole book, just the title), professional fly fishermen Art Lee accuses the typical British trout angler of being 'rather staid'.

One of his techniques is to skitter a large skater over the surface to stir the trout up. When a fish comes to the surface, heart missing beats like crazy, Mr Lee swaps the large skater for a standard pattern.

If the trout refuses to stir at all, he recommends throwing a stone at it to wake it up. He actually did this on the English River Test, the cad. Whatever was happening to the trout, there must have been a few missed heartbeats among the pukka sahibs on the bank.

Picture the scene: after the fumbling for brandy flasks and outbreaks of well-bred curses, the Test resounding to cries of, 'Jeeves! Me horsewhip! On second thoughts – me twelve-bore!' It's a wonder the bounder wasn't thrashed within an inch of his life, or packed off back to the States with an air-conditioned seat to his pants.

Back to the trout, who, after all Mr Lee had skittered over him and thrown at him, should by rights have turned purple and passed over, muttering, 'Keep going, you fool . . .' How did the Aberdeen scientist discover what made his ticker cease to tock.)

(Incidentally, if ever your watch conks out, take it to a German watchmender. Zey heff vays of makink it tock.

(Nothing at all to do with trout, but I've got a bucketful of ancient German jokes I'm trying to use up.)

A battery-powered transmitter was the secret. Humanely implanted, it was, so the trout didn't feel a thing at the time. But back in the water it must have got that sinking feeling. Perhaps that was why it didn't feel like moving far from home.

In case there were any escapees from the experiment, you'd be advised to check any trout you catch around Aberdeen. Trout don't figure in matches, thankfully, or there'd be a few disqualifications at the weigh-in. Battery-powered transmitters might be one up on the tried-and-trusted spiral leads, but they still wouldn't count as a legitimate contribution towards a record weight.

Take extra care too when you're cleaning trout for the pan, or you could give your dentist a few probs. Especially if he insists on asking questions, as dentists usually do, when your mouth is gagged wide open.

'Front tooth missing, eh? And how did we come to do that?'

'Hathewy-howerth thanthmither.'

'Hathewy-howerth thanthmither? What the hell's a hathewy-howerth thanthmither?'

'I hith it. In a thwouth. Hoke my thooth thlean oth.'

'Hoke your thooth thlean oth, eh? A hathewy-howerth thanthmither?'

'Yith.'

'Nurth! . . .'

It is a little-known scientific fact that, when affected by the spectacle of a raving loony rendered thoothleth by a hathewy-howerth thanthmither, the heart of even a dentist will skip a beat.

Take your litter home

I must admit to being a little *distrait*, which I think is French for put out, at the state of the Grand Union towpath when, with Mad Mac and Big McGinty, I made the annual post-Christmas hangover walk.

Perhaps not all of the litter on the bank was left by anglers. But who else would have been daft enough to attempt the Grand Union towpath in that weather? Nor did the three of us add to the attractions of the towpath, but at least we were mobile rubbish. We were not just lying there waiting to be swept up. Not this time, anyway.

Bottles, cans, butties, paper hats and spent crackers, a score of plastic bags - several still almost full of groundbait - chunks of cake, some half-eaten turkey legs, a great hunk of stilton cheese and a full Father Christmas beard lay within a short stretch.

Why the Father Christmas beard, I'll never know. Perhaps the wearer had been handing out the prezzies at the club do, and decided to get an hour in on the bank before he went home. Or perhaps he'd just been sacked from a local store for clouting the kids and had decided to end it all.

The abandoned eatables wouldn't be a long-term problem: wandering doggies, moggies, sparrows and towpath rats would soon see them off. Normally the ducks would have shifted them, but just before Christmas the number of ducks on the Grand Union seems to drop sharply. (Understandably, perhaps, in these hard times, but even so there's never much on 'em.)

All the hardware, however, seemed to indicate that the previous few day's fishing had not been taken seriously by many. Adding to the clutter on the path lay one training shoe, one right welly, and an article of lady person's clothing. The three may not have been connected, but they did indicate that at least two blokes had had to hop it home and that one lady person must have been severely chilled around the boatyard.

Oh, and there was a body. A muffled figure sitting on his basket in the snow, fast asleep, with a half-empty Scotch bottle beside him. His rod was in position, but he wouldn't have been troubled too much by bites: the terminal tackle was swaying gracefully from the bushes on the opposite bank.

Big McGinty caught him as he lurched forward from the basket, headed straight for a damp and icy shock.

'Wakey, wakey!' bawled McGinty. 'All right, me old son?'

The bloodshot eyes blinked painfully against the morning light. (The angler's bloodshot eyes, not McGinty's: his were already used to it.) A toothless mouth opened gungily in the stubble.

'Last train . . .' it croaked.

'Last train?' said McGinty.

'Last trai-hain . . .' croaked the apparition again, 'to San Fernando-o- . . .' and went back to sleep.

We dragged the unconscious songbird on his basket away from the water and wedged him with his back against a tree, leaving his Scotch within easy reach against the time he decided to make it back to San Fernando.

All in all, even after we'd shifted the body, that stretch of towpath was in a right state. And it was only half a mile out of the hundreds in our great British inland waterways system. So in future, lads – not that you had anything to do with it – let's observe a few Keep-The-Towpath-Tidy rules.

Do all your fishing *before* you go to the pub *or* to the club's annual do, not after you've staggered out. However fit and alert you feel, you're not at your best then, especially in the pitch dark. Resist the temptation to try for a fish for the road. Not only do such attempts cause half the tackle to be left on the bank, they also lead to a high incidence of pierced ears, splintered baskets and falling in the water.

Falling into icy water in an emotional state can lead to serious consequences such as death, which can often prove fatal.

Defunct anglers floating about are not only untidy but a hazard to navigation. They are also very boring company for any mates who have to take them home to their Ever Lovings. And they take a bit of explaining: 'I've brought him back in one piece, love, but I'm afraid he's a bit . . . er . . . dead.'

There are ways of breaking it more gently, but one which is *not* recommended is the Irish tactful method, 'Is it the widow Murphy I'm speaking to?'

Non-defunct anglers, splashing around the canal and screaming for help do not do much for the image of the calm waterside philosopher. Especially when they're doing it in only three feet of water.

Not only that: anglers are high on the list of pollutants. It doesn't even need a whole angler: just a pair of angler's feet can have the fish turning belly-up for 200 yards downstream.

Clubs can help by providing a bin or a skip for anglers to dump their rubbish in. Perhaps two skips: one for the rubbish, the other for any anglers who insist on going for a last late-night dangle, but who are too far gone in the Demon Drink to navigate the towpath without risk. At least their loved ones will know where to collect them in the morning.

But in the end, it's up to the anglers. They can help by taking only the essentials onto the bank and making sure they take everything home with them.

'Hello, darling. I've brought everything back from the canal. Look: rod, line, reel, breadpaste, groundbait and – er . . . Oh, I don't believe you've met Miss Maisie Fruit.'

Well, perhaps not *everything* . . .

The Sludgethorpe Diaries

... being extracts from the diaries and other documents of the Sludgethorpe Waltonians. This from the diary of Edward (Big Eddie) Fanshawe, licensee of the *Bricklayer's Arms.*

Big Eddie's quiet Christmas

Since the Sludgethorpe Waltonians made me an honorary member, they've practically taken over the *Bricklayer's*.

I must admit that I wasn't too keen on them at first, especially when they turned up in droves after a match, all dripping and steaming and ponging the place out. Nor was I keen on the antics of such people as Chalky White, Sludgethorpe's ace matchman, who was always plying little darlings with high octane drinks and evil intent. In the past I'd been used to a better class of dirty old man.

It wasn't just the human members I wasn't keen on, either: Harry Turner's ferret really is an acquired taste. My good lady wife still goes funny all over whenever she sees it.

But one day I looked around and realised that practically all my customers were Waltonians. For some reason or other, all the old regulars had disappeared. I didn't mind, really, because the Waltonians supped plenty, and now and again brought back members of opposition teams after a home match.

In the end I had to admit that, like it or not, I was running a fisherman's pub. The brewery had realised this as well, and I heard rumours that they were considering changing its name to something like the *Izaak Walton* or the *Compleat Angler*, repainting the outside and decorating all the way through.

Now, this would do wonders for trade. Let's face it, a name like the *Bricklayer's Arms* and a decor of flock wallpaper and plastic ivy isn't the ultimate in sophistication, and it would be great to pull in some really classy passing trade to top up what the Waltonians were spending.

So I had this great idea to encourage the brewery, to show them that I was thinking along exactly the same lines. I renamed the Saloon Bar the *Creel Room,* and the Public Bar the *Matchman's Mess.* (Highly appropriate, that last one: some of the messes the matchmen take in there have to be seen to be believed.)

I hung the walls with old keep nets, rods, rod rests, landing nets and hung some old wicker baskets from the ceiling. Very tasteful. There were one or two complaints from people who bumped their heads on the baskets, but they got used to them in time.

Pride of place in the Saloon Bar - sorry, the Creel Room - was of course the stuffed pike with which the Waltonians had presented me. But the Matchman's Mess still needed something to finish it off. More stuffed fish, being the price they were, were out of the question. Perhaps some sporting prints? Certainly something with a bit of character...

Character! That was it. It came to me as I was looking at the pimple on Tupper Brown's nose, and wondering how Clogger Sedgewick had come by those missing teeth. There was enough character in the faces of the Waltonians to fill the average Chamber of Horrors ten times over.

I'd have a colour photograph taken of each of them, have it framed and stick it on the wall in the Public - the Matchman's Mess. The members would come in to admire themselves every night and passing strangers would be fascinated by the full horror of the Waltonian line-up. I don't have many ideas, but the ones I do have are real goodies...

I had a word with Ken Scratcher, ace (and only) reporter of the *Sludgethorpe Echo.* Ken said he knew the very man: Sid 'Flash' Gordon, ace (and only) photographer of the *Echo.* Not only would Flash take all the pictures, but he would take them for free, provided I let Ken make a feature of it for the paper.

I was delighted. Free photographs *and* all that free publicity in the *Echo.* And just in time for Christmas. I couldn't go wrong.

So how come I did?

Faces such as adorn the Waltonians do not get that way because the owners have lived lives of solitude and meditation. Faces which look as if they've been sat on while warm, chiselled out of old railway sleepers, hit by a brick or run down by a tram, often get that way because they've been sat on while warm, chiselled out of old railway sleepers, hit by a brick or run down by a tram.

The owners have lived a little, knocked about a bit, *been* knocked about a bit. And in doing so have aroused the odd bit of personal animosity here and there among persons who have been looking for them ever since.

The pictures went up on the wall, and then they went into the *Echo*. A splendid double spread it was, with a banner headline announcing THE FISHERMEN OF SLUDGETHORPE. Underneath each portrait was a caption with a few personal details, and the main story stressed that all these splendid chaps were regulars of the *Bricklayer's*. My own picture, naturally, was in as well.

The very next night, two young ladies came in looking for Chalky White. Separately. It appeared that he'd told each of them that she was the only love of his life. What made it worse when they confronted him, and each other, was that he was looking deep into the eyes of Mrs Lulu Waghorn, young and lovely wife of the former chairman of the Veterans' Committee. Good job Chalky's own missus wasn't there. She really *would* have killed him.

During the following week, we had lots of visits from strangers. The bailiff from Slagville Piscatorials, deadly rivals of the Waltonians, came in looking for three Waltonians who had been fishing Slagville waters on tickets whose names didn't tally with the photographs in the *Echo*.

Four intellectual citizens from the Keep Sludgethorpe White vigilantes, wearing Doc Marten boots and brass-buckled belts, came in looking for Chukkitan Chansit, the little Pakistani Waltonian. They'd have done him some damage if Harry Turner hadn't got in first with a stool.

Harry Turner himself was carted off the next night by two CID men who'd been looking for a bloke catching ducks on a carp rod from Jackson's Clay Pit. The description they had fitted Harry's photograph; possibly because Harry had been catching ducks on a carp rod from Jackson's Clay Pit.

A vanload of ancient Teddy Boys came down in search of Clogger Sedgewick and Tupper Brown, to continue an argument which started in 1959 over the relative merits of Elvis Presley and Jerry Lee Lewis. Talk about *Great Balls of Fire* . . .

After that I lost count. There were re-possession men from hire purchase companies, bailiffs serving writs on the Waltonians for arrears of rent, several more distraught maidens who had been done wrong by various members, assorted grocers and butchers waving unpaid bills and several licensees from outlying areas who had been unwise enough to allow the Waltonians to put booze on the slate. In the end, the Waltonians were just too scared to come in. Even the ones who hadn't been nobbled obviously had something on their consciences. And all because of those pictures in the *Echo*.

So here I am. At Christmas. Which should be the busiest time of the year. Looking at an empty pub. How does that poem go?:

> *'Twas the night before Christmas,*
> *when all through the house*
> *Not a creature was stirring,*
> *not even a mouse . . .*

All it needs now is for someone to come looking for me. I've thrown out some roughnecks from different pubs in my time. There was that Irish navvy I had carted off by the police when I kept the *Pineapple* in Slagville all those years ago. He always swore he'd catch up with me when he came out.

Hey up... the door's opening. First customer of the - eek!

Hush my big mouth...

Hell below zero

Nobody's ever called me a fair weather fisherman.

(Nobody's ever called me a fisherman, but I'm not proud.)

I reckon to be a hard man. Where I was brought up, any kid with two ears was a sissy. But I can't stand the cold.

I was daft enough to want to try out my Christmas wellies. Olive green, calf length and rather dashing. And I'd arranged a session of the Noble Art for the morrow with Mad Mac and Big McGinty.

That night it snowed. And snowed. And snowed and snowed and snowed. I took refuge in the *Boot and Slipper*, where I met old buddy mate Doc Thumper, physician extraordinary and guide and counsellor in moments of stress and impoverishment.

'I'm feeling a little dicky, Doc,' I said.

'At your age you must expect it,' he said. 'Especially in this cold weather. I would recommend a peripheral vascular dilator.'

'Is it painful?'

'No, it's Scotch.'

What a lovely feller.

'Now then. Any other problems?'

I cracked.

'Yes, Doc. I can't face tomorrow. I'll freeze to death. I'll die, I know I will. Tell me I'm not fit.'

'Rubbish. Just what you need. Blow the cobwebs off. Bring the pallor back to your cheeks. I want to hear all about it when you come to Monday's surgery for the frostbite pills. Until then, not another word.'

* * *

First light on the morrow. Plough through snow to garden compost heap, to dig out some prime specimens from the Parker herd of pike-strangling lobs. None of which seem to be around.

Fat lot of use those worms turn out to be. Spend all summer six feet down to escape the drought. Come up for a quick breath of air in the autumn monsoon. And now disappear again beneath the permafrost. All except for this one little beaut- Hey! Bring that worm back at once!

You can go off bloody robins.

'Surprise, surprise!' calls Dearly Beloved. 'Before you go . . . I've got something for your chest.'

For my chest? What can it be? Liniment? Goosegrease? Hair-piece? Living bra?

No. Help! Not – *The Thing!*

Yes, *that*. The Thing which Darling Daughter has been knitting for three months. In red, green and yellow. Fluorescent. Thirty six feet long and varying in width from six to twenty-four inches. Calls it a scarf.

It doesn't go with my wellies. Doesn't go with my Man United bobbly hat. Wouldn't go with anything except a deformed giraffe. But if I refused to wear it, Darling Daughter's feelings would be hurt. So would mine, because Dearly Beloved would fetch me one with the frying pan.

* * *

Pick up Mad Mac. Eek!

Mac wearing *his* Christmas wellies. Iridescent mauve with a watered silk pattern. And on his head a big furry thing. Possibly a cat which has crawled up there and died.

'You are not coming out with me in that lot,' I said, putting my foot down. In my olive green, calf length wellies.

'Prezzies,' said Mac, 'from my Ever Loving. Which I have to wear on pain of being separated from my breath. You can talk: what's that peg rug doing round your neck?'

Fair dos, I suppose. Mac's Cossack hat and my seven-league scarf would help to keep out the cold, which was getting colder by the minute. And it was infinitely preferable to the summer scene when Mac was on his cycling kick and turned out in his Eddie Merckx cap and black satin shorts. Not a pretty sight.

. . . Pick up Big McGinty. Who never feels the cold on account of nineteen stone of insulation, referred to occasionally by unkind persons as blubber. But who is claiming every ailment known to man as a reason for not making the trip.

It is necessary to point out to him very firmly that it is impossible to have high blood pressure and low blood pressure at the same time. That the same goes for flat feet and rising arches. And that dandruff does not qualify as an incapacitating physical disability.

We get to the river in a raging blizzard, reflecting on the hazards and discomforts of angling as a pastime, wishing we were dedicated to crib, dominoes, darts, or perhaps some gentler and more creative pursuits. Making a model of Bo Derek from 500,000 matchsticks, for instance. Or Dolly Parton from 750,000.

Must be firm. We're here to fish and fish we shall. But what's this on our favourite stretch? A hundred and fifty goose-pimpled lunatics fishing a match. Immobile. Half of them probably already dead from the cold, an offence under the match rules and liable to lead to disqualification.

A steward appears and tells us to disappear. And to take our poncy wellies, daft hats and fluorescent scarves with us before we frighten the fish.

Have a care, my good man, or my big friend here will sit on your head, and my little friend here will bite your kneecaps. Yer what? And whose army? You know what you can do with your rule book as well. Page by page.

On that witty and sophisticated riposte, we make our way up to a steep and tree-lined stretch of bank. Difficult to negotiate, but at least away from anti-social stewards and offering some shelter from the Klondike wind.

Mac and I quickly reach the bottom, sliding from tree to tree. We turn to await McGinty. Who is still at the top.

'I can't make it!' he shouts. 'Too steep. Too much snow. Bad leg. Old wound. Hammer toe. Athlete's foot. Poorly finger. Let's go home.'

'Rubbish! Remember you're British! Best foot forward! Down in no time.'

It was possibly not McGinty's best foot, but at least he was down in no time. From top to bottom like a Bunter-sized bobsleigh, saved from a watery grave only by the intervention of a noble willow tree, which would never be the same again.

'Ooooh! Me back! Me front! Me hip flask! Don't let poor Nellie starve. Remember only this of me. That in some corner . . .'

If there's one thing I can't stand it's a bloke who won't die quietly.

Risking pulled fetlocks and treble hernias, Mac and I get

McGinty to his feet, sit him gently on his reinforced stool, tackle up for him and put the rod firmly into his nerveless hand. Then cast out ourselves and wait.

The snow turns to sleet. The sleet turns to rain. The wind changes course and finds us. A big black dog crashes down through the trees, scoffs two of Mac's butties and does a naughty up against McGinty. We have known better days.

'Heads we go home,' says Mac. 'And tails we stay.'

It takes four goes for the coin to come down heads. Even though Mac is tossing.

Up the bank. Tugging and straining at McGinty, who is nowhere near so good at going up as he was coming down. Mac and I by now candidates for intensive care.

Past the matchmen. Who by this time are all on the verge of death from exposure and goosepimple poisoning. A friendly treble raspberry for the steward, who will later have to explain to the wives about the outbreak of sudden death among their match-fishing husbands. And serve him right.

* * *

Heroes we are, back at the *Boot and Slipper.* Walking wounded. Living dead. Shucks, it was nothing. Bit rough. Bit cold. But you get used to that sort of thing when you're as dedicated as we are. And hard men with it. On the house? You're too kind, landlord. Yes, there we were, chipping holes in the ice...

If there's another thing I can't stand, apart from the cold and blokes who won't die quietly, it's telling fibs about fishing trips. Unless it's in a good cause.